Lydia Richter

Baby Dolls

with heads made of bisque from 1909 until circa 1930
Character Baby Dolls

Hobby House Press™

Published by   Cumberland,
Maryland 21502

PUBLISHER:
Lydia Richter

CONCEPTION AND LAYOUT:
Joachim F. Richter

TEXT:
Lydia Richter (except pages 18-23)
Pages 18-23: Anita Eckner and Lydia Richter, Pages 88-91: Karin Schmelcher

PHOTOGRAPHS:
Cover photographs: Lydia and Joachim F. Richter
Alfred Barsotti: pages 15, 32, 40 (above left), 46 (below), 58 (below right), 62 (above left and middle), 74, 78, 79, 88, 89, 93, 95, 108
Auction house Christie's: page 57
Katharina Engels: pages 21, 25 (below left), 36 (above right), 81 (above right), 92 (middle), 96 (below left)
Ulrich Gierse: page 82 (below)
Elke Gottschalk: page 50 (above middle)
Dietrich Graf: pages 6 (above), 24 (above left), 44 (middle), 48, 49, 50 (below middle), 52
Ella Hass: page 15 (below)
H. Mathias Lossnitzer: pages 36 (below left), 41 (middle), 56, 63 (middle), 64, 72, 77, 82 (above), 96 (above left)
Joachim F. Richter: pages 6 (below), 7-9, 10 (above), 12 (above), 13, 18, 22, 23, 24 (far upper left), 25 (above row), 25 (below right), 42, 50 (below right), 62 (below left), 68, 69 (below right), 70, 76, 81 (middle), 85, 86, 89, 91, 94 (below right), 104, 105 (below left)
Lydia Richter: pages 1, 2, 4, 12 (below), 16, 28, 31, 34, 35, 38 (middle), 39 (middle), 41 (above right), 46 (above), 50 (above right), 51, 53, 60, 61, 65, 66, 67, 69 (middle and above right), 71, 73, 75, 84, 87, 98, 99, 100-103, 105 (above and below right), 106 (below left)
Harald Rochelt: pages 26, 29, 33, 55, 58 (above right), 58 (below left), 58 (below middle), 97 (above right), 107 (below)
Hannelore Schenkelberger: pages 25 (middle row), 110
Karin Schmelcher: pages 14, 30, 37, 38 (above left), 58 (above left), 80, 83, 92 (left)
Georg Schrott: page 107 (above left)
Rosemarie Vogelsang: pages 10 (below), 39 (above right), 58 (above middle)

ACKNOWLEDGEMENTS:
The publisher and author wish to thank the following for the loan of dolls and accessories: Alfred Barsotti: auction house Christie's, London; Mrs. Sonja Dallman; Mrs. Anita Eckner; Mrs. Eleonore Gau; Mrs. Doris Giebelhausen; Ulrich Gierse; Mrs. Elke Gottschalk; Doll House Frankfurt, Ralph Knedel; Doll Clinic Renate, Berlin; Doll Museum Katharina Engels, Rothenburg o. T.; Doll Museum Carin Lossnitzer, Coburg; Doll Museum Stein am Rhein, Erika Steiner; Doll Museum Mathias Wanke, Limburg/Lahn; Mrs. Helga Neubeck; Mrs. Reinmund; Mrs. Hannelore Schenkelberger; Mrs. Karin Schmelcher; Mrs. Rotraut Schrott; Mrs. Hildegard Stix; Mrs. Rosemarie Vogelsang; Mrs. Walter.

REFERENCES
The German Doll Industry 1815-1940, Georgine Anke/Ursula Gauder; *The History of Kämmer & Reinhardt in the Mirror of Their Own Description; Blue Book of Dolls & Values*, Jan Foulke; *The Collector's Encyclopedia of Dolls Vol. II*, Coleman; *Armand Marseille Dolls*, Patricia R. Smith; *Histoire et Etude de la S.F.B.J.*, Anne-Marie et Jacques Porot.

Translation: Michael T. Robertson
ISBN 0-87588-331-1
PRINTED IN SPAIN BY EGEDSA
D.L. B- 27722 -88

J.D. Kestner. Neck mark: "J.D.K. 247."

This wonderful side profile of this charming Baby doll shows rather well the exquisite modelling of the face.

Endpapers:
Erika dolls, numbers 1489 from Simon & Halbig (see page 85).

Page 1:
The beloved *Dream Baby* from Armand Marseille in an old hand-stitched baptismal dress.

Table of Contents

A very rare and unusual baby doll from the firm Gebr. Knoch (see page 65), clothed in a beautiful old baby doll dress made of net and lace trimming decorated with silk bows (cape, jacket, bonnet and ornamental shawl).

Introduction

A book about baby dolls? My first thought was that this could possibly be an exciting and interesting topic, as these wishes of my readers were delivered to me. Due to the fact that we had already produced so many doll books, my next thought was would this topic bring enough new and interesting information? Also, would it interest and delight our readers?

Baby dolls have always enraptured me but until now, I have had very little time to delve deeply into this subject. Once I earnestly employed myself with this topic and had a general view of it, I was surprised, even amazed at the imposing varieties of baby dolls. I had the feeling that the doll makers had used all of their experience, knowledge, improvements, new ideas, child-wishes and dreams and embodied these things into their baby dolls. Since the production of the book had been decided upon, I begin this task with new enthusiasm and vigor.

As always, it was my greatest desire to introduce these beautiful baby dolls in large colored photographs so that each detail would be recognized, as well as furnishing a lot of important factual information. The beauty, character and radiance of these baby dolls should be emphasized since they were the reason that these dolls were loved and collected. If one could not feel the magic of these old dolls, then surely the circle of collectors in this world would not continue to grow. To try and impart some of this magic is the main object of this book.

Today these baby dolls are desirable collectors' and museum pieces, but once upon a time they were toys which were loved and cherished by children. Parents bought them for their small daughters to fulfill their Christmas or birthday wishes. Although they were to play with and enjoy those baby dolls, there was a serious thought behind this play. They were preparing for their future responsibilities as mothers.

The contact with so many collectors, as well as auction houses and museums, has bestowed upon us so much knowledge, information and photographic material. In addition, I had the luck in finding so many helpful collectors who made it possible for me to photograph so many beautiful baby dolls. I would especially like to thank them for helping and supporting us in this venture. From this huge variety we chose a cross section of unusual, common and well-known, beautiful, but also realistic and even ugly baby dolls. We wish all of our readers a lot of enjoyment and hope that the collectors will find this book very useful.

Lydia Richter

Play doll cut out of cardboard, circa 1912.

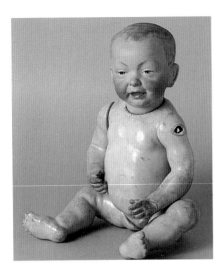

The so-called *Kaiser Baby* from Kämmer & Reinhardt.

Neck mark of the *Kaiser Baby*.

Porcelain baby doll in swaddling clothes. Underside mark: "ges. gesch. 579/1," 4³/₄in (11cm).

Kämmer & Reinhardt Creates the First Realistic Baby Doll

It was the reputable doll factory of Kämmer & Reinhardt, Waltershausen, who around 1909 introduced to the astonished trade world as well as the general public the first realistic looking baby doll. Its head was made of bisque and was molded after a model of an infant. Also for the first time the body was anatomically and realistically reproduced from a model. The doll heads were produced by the porcelain factory of Simon & Halbig, while Kämmer & Reinhardt produced the composition bodies themselves.

The trade world was immediately interested, and many doll manufacturers may have asked themselves why they themselves never came up with this idea, which had long been "hanging in the air." It was not quite understandable that until now the baby doll had been missing among the unbelievable variety of dolls.

The production of dolls with china, and later with bisque heads, had already found its beginning around 1850. At first it was the lady doll creations with their adult-like features which dominated. They were often clothed in long gowns or elegant dresses. Around 1870 they were replaced by other dolls whose features were more child-like. These represented girls between six and twelve years of age.

In only a few decades, these porcelain doll heads developed from simple beginnings into unusual beauty and perfection. As such, it was even more astounding that not until 1909 had a real baby doll existed. Stylistic attempts had been made of different materials such as wood, wax, papier-mâché and from around 1850, also porcelain. These could actually be called the forerunners. Examples of this would be the baby in swaddling clothes, bath dolls and infants to be baptized. The infant to be baptized was called as such due to its clothing; it was dressed only in a long shirt and bonnet which was the way infants were dressed at that time. He had nothing to do with the realistic baby. He had neither a typical baby doll head nor did he have the anatomy of a baby's (reproduced) baby body. Its body was copied from a Japanese doll and is known today as the Motschmann-type body. (See page 7.)

In the years prior to 1909, it was the fashion to dress girl dolls with baby clothes and to sell them as babies. This is especially evident from an article written in an 1880 *Harper's Bazar* in which Kestner's beautiful girl dolls in long baby clothes were exhibited and sold.

So it was that this baby doll, which was created in 1909 by Kämmer & Reinhardt, was the first of its type and a small sensation for the doll market.

How did this come about and what was the cause that started this? Around the turn of the century one noticed a certain tiredness in the doll business. It needed new attractions. In 1908, various doll makers, among them Marion Kaulitz, presented their realistic dolls at a Munich industrial fair. These were called "artist" dolls. The interest of the visitors was great but even so, the general feeling was that some of these dolls were rather ugly and were not very graceful or desirable. Excerpts from the *Berliner Tageblatt*, Berlin's daily paper (1910), read,

"From artists, who bring art into life,...all attention has been steered also upon the toys for children. In contrast to the sophisticated products produced by the modern industry, which so easily confused and bored a child, simple, large forms were created...At last the attention was drawn towards the dolls. For the first time a new attempt was shown at the Munich Fair of 1908. In imitation of old models, especially those of the (characteristically) carved wooden figures of nativity scenes, sculptors modeled (individual) heads for new dolls, which were simply dressed in colorful farmers' costumes or in original children's costumes. They declared war against dolls with expressionless beauty and produced daringly original, but also ugly types..."

Two bath dolls made of china, also called *Frozen Charlottes*, circa 1870. Forerunners of the realistic baby dolls.

These realistic dolls, far removed from the beauty of that time, had been given the decisive push. It was Franz Reinhardt of Kämmer & Reinhardt who sensed his great chance in this development and employed appropriate ideas. One could feel that the summit of beauty and perfection in dolls had already been crossed and that something new had to be produced. Therefore, other paths had to be taken and the idea to produce dolls which had realistic features, like the kids in the neighborhood, was obvious to him. Franz Reinhardt decided to take this risk and found the courage to embark into this business. He called his new dolls character dolls instead of "artist dolls." Baby was the number 100, which stood at the very beginning. This doll head originated from a bronze bust by a Berlin artist who had modeled it after a six-week-old infant. This was written in an authentic company document called "The History of Kämmer & Reinhardt in the Reflection of Their Own Portrayal," which was published on their 25th anniversary. In the meantime, however, we know it was Professor Arthur Lewin Funke who had modeled this head after a six-month-old infant. Baby later received the name *Kaiser Baby*, because it was believed that there were certain traits which were similar to those in infant photographs of the Kaiser. In how far this was correct is impossible to say. However, this doll with

Early wooden doll with Motschmann-type body, circa 1860.

the name *Kaiser Baby* did become famous and well-known throughout the world.

This so-called *Kaiser Baby* was for the taste of that period not pretty and sweet, but the sight of this small and helpless baby had awakened the protective motherly instincts of the onlookers and hardly anyone could resist it. After some initial uncertainties and a lot of apprehension, Kämmer & Reinhardt experienced a great success. Orders came pouring in and the anniversary document of the company stated that the success was unparalleled in the annals of doll production. Of course, one has to add that this great success did not last too long,. The *Berliner Tageblatt* (Berlin daily paper), January 25, 1914, tells us:

"the character dolls were a great mistake made by artists and manufacturers. The general public soon rejected them with amazing unanimity, and by this date they have completely disappeared. These dolls only received a short revival due to the fact that their appearance was softened and they looked more and more like to the old doll heads. A very special well-known shop in Berlin had a turnover of the original character dolls when they had first appeared and still had an attraction of being new of around ten percent of their complete sales. In the following years, their sales continually sank until in 1912, they were just three percent. However, when in 1913 Ursula with the long curls appeared for the first time in the shop windows, a very special mixture between a character doll and an old doll, so to speak a beautiful character doll, the sale of these dolls increased to approximately forty percent. The old character dolls, with minor exceptions, were not kept or requested. The moderate character dolls which were kept in stock only brought about twenty percent of the complete sales.

"An indirect offspring of the artist doll was the baby. It had more success and had developed far more strongly than its older sisters, the character dolls, but it also had its own peculiarities. It was found while searching for a characteristic child's head and its model was a bronze bust of a six-week-old baby. The effect of this head was ugly when reduced in scale from bronze to celluloid or bisque without the artist's hand and produced by thousands of dozens out of a mold. Like an embryo in a test tube, this baby creature strikes us rather strangely, like an old withered person whose teeth were not supposed to grow but had long since fallen out. When they were plump and well-nourished, they had a strange similarity to cretons. From the very beginning, these babies had great success and are still very popular today. They were presented to the general public for the first time by a company at the first Redoute Fridericiana. They immediately found 200 admirers who were

A small metal baby wagon with an all-bisque 4in (10cm) doll, circa 1920.

willing to pay 20 marks per baby. The triumphant success of this baby with its bent legs and compact infant body was not due to its head, but in spite of it. The manufacturers became wise very quickly after their failure with character dolls; they molded their infant's head more and more according to the laws of beauty of the old dolls. As soon as the general public was offered a lovelier baby head, they ignored the old and ugly heads. Even today prettier dolls are still preferred.''

This development leads to only one conclusion: the realistic character dolls were favored more by the manufacturers and parents who wanted an artist doll with high quality, but they had forgotten to ask the children whether they liked their new toy companions. One had written the bill without the host — or in this case, the children. The children were the ones who received the dolls as presents to be played with and enjoyed. Parents who spent a lot of money for a toy did not wish to have a disappointed child, which surely was often the case, especially when a small, ugly, bald head was found under the Christmas tree instead of a blonde curly-haired baby doll. So the buyers began to purchase the dolls which would please the children — the pretty dolls with sleep eyes and wigs. Today the collectors have already shown their delighted opinion about these character babies — artistically valuable, realistic, lovable and highly worth collecting.

The longest running sales success must have been by Kämmer & Reinhardt with their baby number 126, which according to the catalog was called *My Favorite Baby*. It hardly agrees with the ideas of reality and character but it is so charming, that in the past as well as today, it has especially appealed to many buyers as well as collectors. Today these dolls are still found rather frequently; definitely a sign that large numbers of them were sold. Documentation about this doll's popularity is still to be found in the last catalogs of Kämmer & Reinhardt. As such one can read the following advertising slogan in the catalog from 1927: "My Favorite Baby, the world's first and loveliest doll — copied by all — but never matched." Besides the number 126 *My Favorite Baby*, there were only two other character babies to be found in this catalog, the models number 127 and number 128 (the latter also came with a celluloid head which was marked with the number 728).

The catalog of 1930 was still dominated by the number 126 *My Favorite Baby* but no trace of the other character baby sisters was to be found. It was shown in the cover photograph with a pigtail wig. The 126 was offered in many versions — with sleep eyes, with eyelashes or flirting eyes, with the eye mechanism called "Der Unart" (naughty), with movable tongue and with a fine mohair wig. Its head was made either of bisque, composition or celluloid, and was equipped with the

Neck mark of a rare baby from Kämmer & Reinhardt (see page 50, top row, middle).

Three little bisque men in a tub.

A fascinating child doll, only marked with number 149. Socket head on a toddler body.

following bodies: bent-limb baby, standing-stitting baby, toddler or a slender straight-leg body without joints in elbows or knees.

Now back to the year 1909. After the initial great success of the *Kaiser Baby*, no manufacturer wanted to miss the opportunity of profiting from the trends of the time. Therefore, they started to produce, as fast as possible, a baby doll themselves. There was so much heavy competition that some companies copied the successful character doll of Kämmer & Reinhardt, forcing Franz Reinhardt to conduct several lawsuits, which he won. As the company reports, their character doll heads enjoyed the protection of the law, according to the copyright law of works of fine art. Franz Reinhardt had the right that replicas could be confiscated, but being a noble businessman, he never made use of his rights. Onc thing he did achieve was to halt the copying of his character dolls.

Baby doll from Baehr & Proeschild. Neck mark: "582-7," circa 1915.

Other Successful Doll Manufacturers

The doll manufacturers who were warned by the lawsuits began designing other models, so that a great number of new baby-types in all skin colors and many different versions were developed. Unfortunately, the lawsuits could not completely prevent many doll manufacturers from copying the successful dolls of other companies.

Among the manufacturers there was one company in particular, the Gebrüder Heubach, which stood out. With their never-ending varieties of character heads, they won undying fame in the world of doll lovers and collectors. There was no fear of ugliness or of the grotesque. They produced a unique number of doll heads with earnest, laughing, crying, sulking and pouting faces. Among the lovely Heubach babies was *Baby Stuart*, a "star" which is introduced on page 43.

Also, the large and successful Kestner doll factory is especially worth mentioning. After being initially inspired by the character dolls of Kämmer & Reinhardt, they produced a large number of their own prominent models, among which especially the baby *Hilda* (see page 59) and the Oriental baby number 243 (see page 62) stood out. Today these are still two of the most desirable dolls for all collectors. *Hilda* combines realism and beauty in an excellent form, which was and is her secret of success. Also, *Hilda* was often copied, just like the *Kaiser Baby, My Favorite Baby* and other successful dolls. These copied similar dolls but were differentiated from their original models by using the word "type;" for example, *Hilda*-type, *Kaiser*-type, and so forth.

Also, rather successful was the porcelain factory of Hertel, Schwab & Co., Stutzhaus, which produced wonderful doll heads. This company was founded in 1910 and as a rule they marked their doll heads not with their name or initials, but only with numerals (mold and size numbers), and very often with the addition, "Made in Germany." The company's name did not appear and that is the reason that this company is relatively unknown today. Since other companies also marked their dolls with numerals, quite a few of the doll heads from Hertel, Schwab & Co., were, therefore, credited to other producers, especially Kestner.

A story in itself are the very beautiful, exotic baby dolls, which with their colorful and fanciful dresses, set happy accents in the doll world. Nearly all of the large as well as many of the smaller doll makers produced them, although they were seldom sold in Germany and were mainly intended for export. The reason why they did not sell

The Heubach Sun, a registered trademark of the Gebr. Heubach.

made
M in Germany 16
237
J.D.K. Jr.
1914
©
Hilda

Neck mark of *Hilda* from J.D. Kestner.

152

Neck mark of Hertel, Schwab & Co.

Baby doll from Franz Schmidt (see also page 81) with sleep eyes; below the same head with painted eyes on the cover of a porcelain box.

Neck mark of *Hanna* from Schoenau & Hoffmeister.

in Germany was the fact that no one wanted black baby dolls. In a period when people rarely went on long trips, the children in Germany seldom knew people with different colored skin and, therefore, they were rather foreign to them. That is why a small doll-mother playing her mother-child roll could hardly identify with a black baby. So these black babies were mainly meant for children in other countries who, still at that time, owned colonies, and for America, which was always known for being inhabited with people of many races and skin colors.

Unfortunately, the production of these black baby dolls by the doll manufacturers was in general, rather simple. Mostly, they took their already available dolls and gave them a colored skin tone, without going to too much trouble in designing new models in which the racial characteristics of the face were defined, which was often done with large doll-sisters. Merely the coloring, eyes, wigs and clothing made the transformation.

To foster the success from the very start of these black babies, the loveliest and best-sold dolls were at first chosen to receive a new colored skin tone; for example, among those chosen were the *Kaiser Baby* (only in small quantities), the *My Favorite Baby* number 126 from Kämmer & Reinhardt as well as the *Bye-Lo Baby* to be transformed into cute little black babies. *Hanna* from Schoenau & Hoffmeister was transformed into a Polynesian, by using colored skin and the *Dream Baby* from Armand Marseille even appeared in three versions: white, black and as an Oriental baby, the latter being named *Ellar Baby*.

Among the few manufacturers which showed the characteristic negroid features, Ernst Heubach, Köppelsdorf, produced a pair of beautiful doll heads. The model number 399 especially (see page 40) belonged to these. In addition, this doll was offered with red-brown skin and plaited black hair as a small and charming American Indian baby. It is a great pity that this doll is so very rare.

Besides the many babies with bald heads, painted hair, molded hair, molded-on bonnets or with open crown head and wig, with different skin colors, with painted, intaglio or glass eyes are the mechanical or half-mechanical babies, which are especially worth mentioning. Many of these babies could call "Mamma," "Pappa" or "Mimi," scream or squeak because of a voice-box placed in their chests. Sometimes the crown of the head was cut out and a tone-box was placed into the head. Also, babies with molded-on tears were produced, and others which could cry real tears (a rubber hand pump and tube could press out tears). In addition, there were babies which could drink out of a bottle or wet themselves. Others were able to walk, crawl or clap their hands together. These mechanical devices were activated either through a wind-up compression spring or through pressure on a driving-gear. The simplest mechanism was, of course, the sleep eyes, but there were also the more complicated flirting eyes (side-glancing eyes) as well as the eye mechanism, Der Unart (naughty) found in the *My Favorite Baby* from Kämmer & Reinhardt. If one turned the head or the whole doll towards the right, a pin would fall forward which then blocked the eyes from closing, even when one laid the baby down. Only when one turned it towards the left would the pin recede, allowing the doll to close its eyes and sleep, which meant that the baby was once again behaving itself.

As signs began to show the downfall of the porcelain doll industry in the 1920s, there followed once more a brief flourishing of the production of baby dolls with the so-called newborn look. Actually, this type was already conceived in 1909 with the *Kaiser Baby*. It showed a bit of the wrinkled facial features of a very small baby and many other companies produced these small bald heads; however, the true success of these dolls did not occur until around the beginning of 1920. The customers, as a rule until then, only bought those somewhat large and prettier babies with sleep eyes and wigs.

Not until the great success of Grace Putnam's *Bye-Lo* did one begin to become aware of the baby doll popularity in Germany. Manufacturers immediately rushed to move with the doll fashions and started to intensify their production of newborn-type babies. It was especially Armand Marseille with the *Dream Baby* who had so much success. The *Dream Baby* became very popular not only in Germany, but also in America, and that is why today one can find this doll rather frequently and it is, as well, a desired collector's piece.

This short flourishing period of the German doll industry did not change the fact that the great era of porcelain doll heads was slowly coming to an end. The export to America stagnated and the consumer began buying more and more of the less expensive unbreakable dolls made from other materials. After 1930, the large doll companies were themselves forced either to change their production or close down.

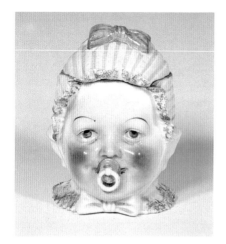

Porcelain cup with removable top.

A.M.
Germany
341./4

Neck mark of *Dream Baby* from Armand Marseille.

The Transformation Capabilities of a Baby Doll

Model head.

A few readers will ask the question, why do so many photographs of dolls in this baby doll book depict small children rather than babies? To this question, a detailed answer will be given.

The production of a very good doll head had always been an expensive and time-consuming business. If it was necessary to produce a new doll head model, it was easier to buy a finished child's bust, as long as one was lucky in finding one which would satisfy all the requirements. Ideal for this was the example of the famous Fiamingo head which anyone could buy inexpensively as a plaster cast at the turn of the century. It has been established that it had been the model of Käthe Kruse's first doll and probably also for a number of dolls with bisque heads such as the number 115 and the 119 baby from Kämmer & Reinhardt, *Fany* from Armand Marseille and others, whose similarities with the Fiamingo head were not wholly accidental.

If it was not possible to find a suitable finished model head, a sculptor was then commissioned to sculpt a doll head. Apart from the baby dolls of the newborn-type, a somewhat older baby as a model was often chosen so that later the doll head created could be used in various ways. The model could be a real baby, such as was the case of the so-called *Kaiser Baby*, or a portrait or painting could be used as a model, as for example *Baby Stuart*. In one particular case, a death mask of a child was used as a model, namely with the Käthe Kruse baby *Dreamer*.

When the baby bust was available, the molds of this doll head were produced. It has already been mentioned that such a doll head was very expensive and so it is obvious that the doll manufacturers tried to use it as much as possible. There were so many transformation possibilities. Apart from the fact that each doll head came out of the mold slightly different and that the hand-painting was never exactly the same, one could make either a boy or girl out of a baby, depending on clothing or hairstyle. A few more examples of the transformation capabilities of a baby head model are: small baby or newborn (Age: a few days to weeks to several months old), head with a closed crown dome, molded hair, painted hair or glued-on fluffy hair, painted eyes or inserted glass eyes, a typical bent-limb baby body baby doll, approximately one year old, the same head as before, but now with an open crown dome and a baby wig, glass sleep eyes, and now with a straight-leg baby body (bent arms and straight legs), a small child up to approximately four years old, the same head as before with open crown dome and a wig with long curls or pigtails, glass sleep eyes, toddler body (small child with jointed body).

Some companies also provided smaller sized heads with baby bodies and larger sized heads with jointed bodies.

The baby dolls were then dressed in appropriate clothing corresponding to their age, with short or long clothes for a baby and later with a playsuit or a shorter dress for a child. Thus, the clothing was a suitable and useful means to perfect the transformation.

As if this was not enough, sometimes a model mold would be slightly changed, or another mold would have an open mouth instead of a closed mouth (or vice-versa), and each time a different new doll head model was created, it usually received a different mold number. An important element was the shape of the eyes. Large round shaped eyes were made for European dolls, while slanted and narrow shaped eyes in very dark colors and a yellowish skin tone created an Oriental baby doll. The best example of this was the *Dream Baby* on page 71. Black babies were simply made by giving them a darker skin color and painting the full lips red (see the *Dream Baby*, page 70). They were often provided with a raven-black curly hair wig. Today there are a few collectors who cannot believe that so many dolls with different appearances were produced from the same master mold.

In the Kämmer & Reinhardt company's business magazine from 1910, one can read that over a period of 23 years, 1886 to 1909, this company dominated this market with only one model. On pages 42 through 45, the examples of the transformation capabilities of a baby doll are shown.

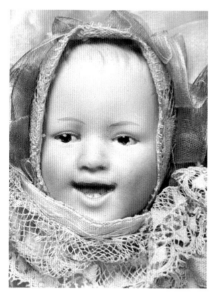

Heubach baby doll (also see page 46).

Heubach girl with same head as above.

A Few Words on the Original Condition of Dolls

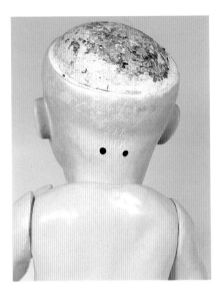

Back of head of a Kestner baby which still has its original plaster dome, with casted neck mark.

made
in Germany
J.D.K.
211

Collectors and lovers of old dolls who have bought a doll or want to buy one are naturally very interested that it is in a good and authentic condition. With so much love for this hobby and apart from the ideal value, no one wants to loose any part of his investment. In the meantime, it is commonly known that a doll with a bisque head combined with the wrong body has far less value. So the question is raised, "When is a doll original and when not?" Original is the condition of the doll when it was sold for the first time. This includes not only the head and body, but also the wig and clothing, including the shoes and socks. Apart from the clothing, which at one time or another existed or still partially exists, it is very possible that head or body, legs or arms have at one point been exchanged.

There are a few rare cases where the doll's origin is immediately identified, namely when the head and body is produced and marked by the same company. (This was sometimes the case with dolls from Kestner), assuming, however, that the head and body fitted together in size, material and color and that they came from the same period, and color as well as the type of body corresponded (for example, black head on a black body, baby head on a baby body). If, however, a doll is not sufficiently marked or known, it is very difficult to establish its originality.

Not too long ago one spoke of original bodies from Armand Marseille, Simon & Halbig or Heubach — only to mention a few examples. A wide spread opinion dominated that these dolls were completely produced in these factories. However, today one has come to realize that the porcelain factories seldom fabricated their own doll bodies in addition to making porcelain bodies. They were, as a rule, suppliers of the porcelain bisque doll heads and doll parts for many other doll factories, often small family businesses, which on their part produced bodies, wigs, doll eyes, clothing and so forth. These doll factories also carried out active trading between each other. Others were satisfied with ordering all the components and completing the dolls.

Larger doll factories like Kämmer & Reinhardt and Heinrich Handwerck had their own doll head molds in their porcelain factories and did not allow other firms to use the heads made from these molds. These heads were usually marked with the name, initials or trademark of the ordering company, sometimes in addition to that of the producing porcelain factory. There were also doll head models which could be obtained by all manufacturers. They were often only marked with the name, initials or trademark of the producing porcelain factory (frequently the case with Gebrüder Heubach and Armand Marseille), but sometimes only with letters or numerals (mostly mold number and size mark) or quite often without any markings. To be informed about the original condition of the latter doll, one must know exact details of how the companies traded among themselves. This is not always possible due to the immense variety of dolls. So today the rule is generally applicable to the old porcelain head dolls — if the head and body are from the same period and the size, material, color and type fit together, they are considered to be original. Several bits of information about the important porcelain factories and the important doll factories who were supplied follow:

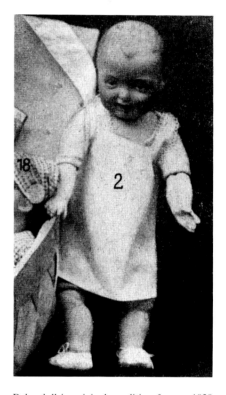

Baby doll in original condition from a 1920 book.

The porcelain factory of Alt, Beck & Gottschalk, Nauendorf near Ohrdruf/Thüringia, supplied C. M. Bergmann, George Borgfeldt, Wagner & Zetzsche and others. The porcelain factory of Baehr & Proeschild, Ohrdruf/Thüringia, supplied Kley & Hahn, Bruno Schmidt and others. The porcelain factory Hertel, Schwab & Co., Stutzhaus near Ohrdruf, supplied Kley & Hahn, Koenig & Wernicke, Strobel & Wilken, George Borgfeldt and others. The porcelain factory Ernst Heubach, Köppelsdorf, supplied Cuno & Otto Dressel, Gebrüder Ohlhaver (Revalo), Adolf Wislizenus, A. Luge & Co. from Sonneberg and others. The porcelain factory Gebrüder Heubach, Lichte/Thüringia, supplied Cuno & Otto Dressel, Hamburger, Wagner & Zetzsche, Eisenmann & Co. and others. J. D. Kestner, Waltershausen, produced their own complete dolls as well as supplying other manufacturers with doll heads and parts as, for example, C. M. Bergmann, Catterfelder doll factory, George Borgfeldt, Kley & Hahn (Ohrdruf/Thüringia), Louis Wolf & Co., Century Doll, Horsman and others.

The porcelain factory Armand Marseille, Sonneberg/Thüringia, supplied Cuno & Otto Dressel, C. M. Bergmann, Otto Gans, Louis Amberg, George Borgfeldt, Louis Wolf & Co. and others. The porcelain factory Schoenau & Hoffmeister supplied the firms Cuno & Otto Dressel, E. Edelmann, E. Knoch, H. Süssenguth and others. The porcelain factory Simon & Halbig, Grafenhain/Thüringia, supplied Kämmer & Reinhardt entirely with character doll heads. As a rule, these doll heads had the size number marked as well as the marking of the company (see the example, left). The number 28 designates the size, which means the doll is 11in (28cm) tall. All the character doll heads from Kämmer & Reinhardt with bodies from

Heinrich Handwerck are also absolutely original since Kämmer & Reinhardt purchased Heinrich Handwerck in 1902 and naturally used the Heinrich Handwerck bodies for their own doll heads. Heinrich Handwerck continued to be independent and was supplied further by Simon & Halbig, just like Franz Schmidt & Co., Cuno & Otto Dressel, Adolf Huls, George Borgfeldt, Gimbel Brothers and others.

Baby Doll Heads

Of very great interest to collectors of antique dolls today are the bisque heads; this is most likely due to the life-like qualities of this material. Important information concerning the production and manufacture can be found in the markings on the back of the head or on the shoulder plate of the doll. The companies used different methods: several marked with their complete names, such as Simon & Halbig and Armand Marseille, while others only used their initials, numerals (mold and size number), some with patent number, letters or with symbols (registered trademark or manufacturer's mark) or they were not marked at all. As far as it is known, Gebrüder Heubach and Swaine & Co., were the only ones who sometimes used a green ink stamp to mark their dolls. Due to the international tariff agreement of 1890, dolls to be exported had to be marked with the country of origin, for example, "Made in Germany." As a rule, the porcelain factories only used porcelain bisque for their doll heads. This was an unglazed white porcelain which could be painted after the first firing with the skin color, be it in pale pink, yellow for Orientals, brown, red-brown or black tones. After this, the cheeks, mouth, eyebrows and

Doll heads, so-called unrefined (or raw) or white product.

lashes, and hair for the bald heads could be painted and the head was then fired a second time.

So far as is known, only Gebrüder Heubach used a pinkish colored porcelain. The first realistic baby head made of porcelain bisque (shortened to bisque) was the head of the so-called *Kaiser Baby*, which is introduced and described on pages 48 and 49. We know of three to four types of heads with baby dolls: socket head with a conical progressing, swivel neck. It is found mainly on composition bodies and can be attached in various ways — for example, heads with an ·open crown had either a wooden disc or a ball placed inside to which a hook (also called an anchor) was attached. This was then hooked to elastic, which in turn connected the arms and legs to the body. With the closed dome socket head a spiral shaped spring with an anchor was screwed into the neck and was attached to the elastic.

On the head with molded-on shoulders, the shoulder head, head, neck and shoulder plate is a complete form and the head cannot be turned. It was attached to the torso either by gluing or sewing it on. The flange neck head was developed in 1922 especially for the soft cloth bodies. Its ring-like connection below the neck was bound into the cloth.

A lot of baby heads are bald heads which show no opening in the head. Therefore, they are referred to as a closed crown dome or head. They have either painted or molded hair, or both. They rarely have fluffy hair with which fine strands of mohair or human hair were glued onto the head. In addition, some companies had baby wigs for the bald heads. The older-looking babies with an open crown dome were very popular and had the pate closed with a cardboard or plaster top and covered with a wig. So far as is known, only Kestner closed their doll heads with a plaster top, and that is why these distinguishing details are important today for those insufficiently marked dolls.

Bald heads often have painted eyes and occasionally intaglio or fixed glass eyes. The intaglio eyes were a speciality of the Gebrüder Heubach. The iris' and pupils of these eyes are indented, which gives them a very natural look. Sleep eyes were used a little later; at the very beginning there were some problems with mounting them into the inside of closed heads. Lead weights allowed the sleep eyes to either open or close, depending upon posture or position of the doll. It is much rarer to find flirting eyes as this mechanism was far more complicated. It consists of two wired frames which were affixed within the head with plaster. The one frame made the eyes move from left to right while the other one opened or closed the eyelids. This mechanism was only placed into heads with an open crown.

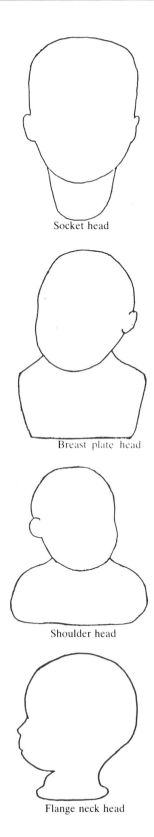

Socket head

Breast plate head

Shoulder head

Flange neck head

A rare baby doll from Simon & Halbig, number 22. Socket head on a bent-limb body, open mouth with two upper teeth, 18¹/₈in (46cm), circa 1915.

Baby dolls could have closed, open/closed or open mouths. They could look earnest, laugh, cry, grimace or open the mouth wide, as if wanting to scream. With the closed mouth the lips are molded together. The lips with the open/closed mouth were molded apart, but between these there was no opening into the inside of the head where a molded mouth cavity could exist — sometimes with molded-on teeth, gums and tongue (see page 46, above right). The open mouth usually had teeth above, but rarely below; the teeth were specially made out of milk glass or porcelain. They could also have either a fixed or movable tongue. The movable tongue of porcelain or compound was affixed to the inside of the forehead with a long brass rod attached with plaster.

For a while babies with molded-on painted bonnets were in fashion. Quite often the bonnets were decorated with flowers. One of the most desirable of these was *Baby Stuart*. This doll was not only available with a molded-on bonnet, but also with a removable molded porcelain bonnet. This had a hole on either side so that a silk ribbon could be passed through and tied.

The two or three-faced baby doll which is rare today was available in various versions. For example, the swivel head could have two or three faces — one which was laughing, one crying and one sleeping. Only one face could be seen at a time, since the others were hidden under a bonnet. When the head was revolved, the wanted face appeared. The other version is a two-face doll which had a white and a black face.

The doll manufacturers were always taking great trouble to invent something new and thus making the child dolls more desirable.

Baby Doll Bodies*

*) Body charts on page 24.

The following introduction concerns the most important different types of baby bodies between 1909 until around 1935. Those made of composition included the bent-limb baby body, the straight-leg baby body, the toddler body and the newborn body, also the leather baby body, the porcelain baby body and the cloth baby body.

The composition bodies are no doubt the most famous and the most widespread. This compound mainly consisted of wood, clay and chalk although some individual companies added and mixed other ingredients according to secret recipes. It was pressed and dried in molds and then finally glued together. The seams which run along the sides had to be smoothed and polished. The separate molded hands were then attached to the arms. All of the parts were finished so that they could be painted with pinkish, yellowish, brown, red-brown or black color. The better quality lighter colored doll bodies received a light touch of pink color make-up on the elbows, hands, knees and feet, as well as painted nails on hands and feet. Finally, all parts were covered with a lacquer, either matte, half-matte or shiny, to make them waterproof.

The production of papier-mâché doll bodies was a less involved procedure. Prefabricated cardboard was pressed into the molds and then stapled together. This type of body was mainly used for inexpensive dolls. Since bodies were so light, they were readily used for export dolls.

Most of the manufacutrers were very meticulous about the production of their doll bodies and were very precise in making them. For example, Kämmer & Reinhardt used a life-like baby body, designed and modeled by sculptors, for their own so-called *Kaiser Baby*. This bent-limb baby body was made of composition had a small tummy and a very lovely well-formed back. The arms were bent, the right one slightly more, the palm of the right hand turned towards the body, while the left one was slightly turned outwards. The middle and ring finger were stuck together, while the forefinger and pinky were spread slightly apart. Arms and legs had disc joints and were attached to the body with elastic. The legs had small fat rolls on the thighs, chubby well-molded knees, well-pronounced calves and baby feet with up-turned large toes. The left leg was drawn up more than the right one. The whole body looked life-like and, in fact, one could imagine this body belonging to a very small child.

Also, the baby bodies of Kestner were of very good quality. However, these bodies are rather similar to the K★R bodies, except

Doll baby with only the neck mark "DJ." Socket head with composition toddler body, 12¹/₈in (32cm).

Body mark of a doll body made by Heinrich Handwerck. Since this company was taken over by Kämmer & Reinhardt in 1902, one will find doll heads from Kämmer & Reinhardt with bodies from Heinrich Handwerck in original condition.

A small baby doll from F & W Goebel. Neck mark: "WG" (below a crown). Made in one piece of bisque, 3³/₈in (9cm).

Body mark on composition toddler bodies from J.D. Kestner.

Body mark on leather bodies from J.D. Kestner.

that the left arm and the right leg are more drawn up and the large toes are not as strongly upturned.

A little later the bent-limb baby body was joined with the straight-leg baby body. This new baby doll was to approximate a one-year-old child. It had a child-like body in contrast to the infant body since it had straight and sturdy legs on which it could stand. Another change was the baby bodies which had a mamma voice. For this, a hole was made in the body for the voice, or it was simply sawed open and the opening concealed with a pink-colored linen tape after the insertion of the voice mechanism.

The body of the newborn child was created around the beginning of the 1920s. With its round back and the socket head set deeply into the body, this doll had the appearance of being very touching and helpless. Arms and legs were bent, just like with all other baby bodies. The hands were mainly balled into a fist; sometimes one or two fingers were pointing. The thumb was spread apart so that it could be stuck into the mouth for sucking. The toddler body (a small child's body) was a jointed body which had joints in the elbows and knees and quite often, wrist joints in addition to the usual joints in the upper part of the arms and legs.

The leather baby body is one of the rarest baby bodies. It consists of a leather torso, leather upper arms and leather thighs. The lower arms and hands, as well as calves and feet, were made in one piece out of composition. These parts were put together using wire and rivets in such a way that the limbs remained movable. Instead of using the usual fine kid leather, oilcloth was sometimes used. It was not as durable, but far cheaper. The filling was usually sawdust, sometimes mixed with cork, or only cork, seaweed or straw. These bodies, which often were more squat and child-like than the usual leather bodies, were fitted with either a baby breast plate or shoulder head or a baby socket head.

The porcelain baby bodies made of bisque are found as a bent-limb baby body or as a straight-leg baby body. As a rule they are not larger than 9¾in (25cm). In many cases the torso and the head were molded in one cast. The arms and legs had disc or ball joints which fitted into the respective cavities of the torso and were bound by elastic or wire, the latter being found used on little dolls.

There are also baby dolls which were casted completely in one mold out of porcelain. Naturally, these do not have movable arms or legs. Porcelain bodies are very captivating, due to their well-defined modeling, but they were and are still very breakable. That is why today one finds only a few of these lovely porcelain baby dolls. Nearly all the manufacturers produced these lovely dolls. The most significant of these were Kestner, Simon & Halbig, Alt, Beck & Gottschalk and Heubach.

At the beginning of the 1920s, the baby doll with a cloth body appeared for the first time. It was an immediate success because it was soft and cuddly and, therefore, very popular. This body was available in many different versions. The most well-known of these was the body of the *Dream Baby*. Its body, arms, legs and feet were made of cotton cheesecloth (muslin). The hands were made of either composition or celluloid. This body came either with or without a mamma voice and was available in many colors, from white to yellow to pink and brown. Arms and legs were slightly bent and were attached with a simple seam or sewn on. The feet were either cut out from cloth in one piece with the legs or were hinted at with an extra sewn-in gusset.

Also known are the cloth bodies with lower arms and legs made of composition. They were attached to the body by thread. The loveliest cloth body was made with round disc joints which allowed it to sit properly and raise and lower its arms. Arms, legs and bodies have round cardboard discs on their joints which were connected using splints. Flange neck heads were tied to these cloth bodies. These were very often produced by Armand Marseille, but also many other porcelain companies made them.

Unfortunately, only very few manufacturers of doll bodies marked their products. Known for this were J. D. Kestner, Heinrich Handwerck, Cuno & Otto Dressel, Koenig & Wernicke and Franz Schmidt & Co. (see markings at the right). Doll bodies were not regularly marked by these manufacturers, and often those with a trademark or label have over the years either faded, washed off or in some other way disappeared.

It has been generally observed that buying a porcelain head doll with an old body, even in bad condition, is far more preferred than a new doll body. In this case a suitable price reduction is usual. Small color abrasions or splintering, scraped fingers and other small damages are not usually reason to reduce the price and this has not held the real collectors back from buying them.

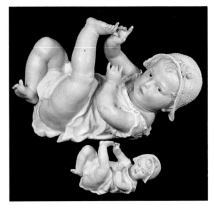

Two piano babies from Gebr. Heubach. Neck mark: (Heubach sun). Intaglio eyes, bonnet and dress are molded onto the body and head, large baby 10⅛in (26cm), small baby 4⅜in (11cm).

Two body marks from Cuno & Otto Dressel.

Body mark from Koenig & Wernicke.

Body marks from Franz Schmidt & Co.

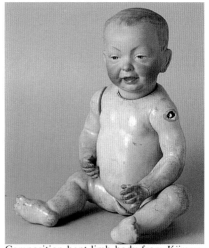

Composition bent-limb body from Kämmer & Reinhardt.

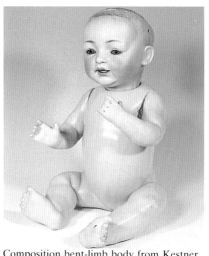

Composition bent-limb body from Kestner.

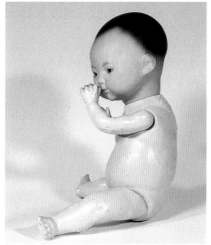

Composition newborn baby body.

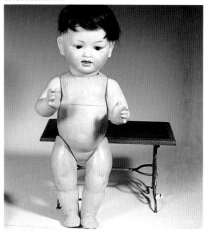

Straight leg baby body from Koenig & Wernicke.

Composition toddler body.

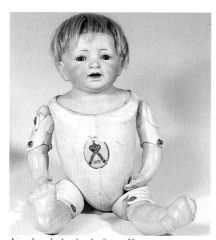

Leather baby body from Kestner.

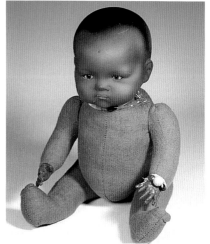

Cloth baby body.

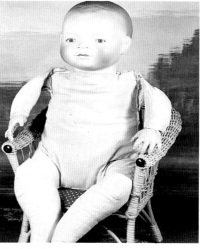

Cloth body from *Bye-Lo*.

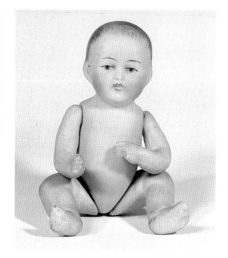

Bent-limb baby body made of bisque.

The *Kaiser Baby* in an old wrought iron cradle.

Metal beds, 4³/₄in (12cm) long, circa 1920, with dolls.

Metal bed with a painted medallion, 9⁷/₈in (25cm), circa 1920.

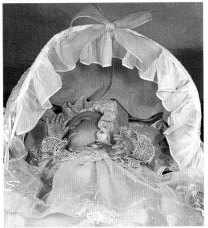

Wicker baby basket with a sleeping *Bye-Lo*.

Wicker baby buggy, circa 1900, with a baby doll.

Metal doll buggy, 5¹/₈in (13cm), circa 1910.

French wicker buggy, 23⁵/₈in (60cm), circa 1860, with an unmarked baby doll.

Three-wheeled wicker buggy with a baby doll marked with the number 122 from Kämmer & Reinhardt.

Baby Dolls for America

Tynie Babe. Neck mark: "E. I. Horsman 1924 made in Germany," 8¾in (22cm).

One of the most interesting chapters in the book of the German doll industry is without a doubt the story of porcelain head dolls and heads which were produced in Germany for export to America. To estimate how extensive this exporting was between 1880 and 1930, one has to be reminded that a huge continent was supplied by two countries, mainly from Germany and in far smaller quantities, France. Kämmer & Reinhardt, for example, maintained showrooms in New York, Mexico, Havana, Buenos Aires and Santiago de Chile in 1927. The statement that this was the largest porcelain doll exporting trade of all time may not be exaggerated.

It is correct in saying that America was called a country of unlimited possibilities. The orders to the German doll manufacturers must have also been nearly unlimited. Those who were lucky to receive large orders could in a very short time become wealthy. This is clearly seen in the historical portrayal of the family of Heinrich Handwerck in which Minna Handwerck, Heinrich Handwerck's wife, talked about her life which was very closely woven to the company's history. According to it, she married in 1884 and lived at first in a small modest apartment. In that same year Heinrich Handwerck became self-employed by selling joke articles and curly braids for wigs. The Handwercks started on the lowest rung of the career ladder but after one year of hard work, Heinrich quickly climbed the ladder and they moved into larger quarters. They started producing dolls with lovely shoulder heads of bisque. In 1886, they moved again after they had received the first order from America and shortly after this, a second order came from Hinrichs & Co., New York. Further larger orders arrived and in 1888, Heinrich Handwerck bought a fashionable house with a very large piece of ground on which he built a long two-storied factory building. Later it was raised, built-on and expanded. This incredible rise would not have been possible without the orders from America.

The buyers of American importing companies like ARRanBEE, George Borgfeldt, B. Illfelder & Co., Strobel & Wilken and Louis Wolf & Sons, only to mention a few, came to Germany and proceeded to visit the showrooms of the doll manufacturers so that they could make their selection. They chose from among the loveliest dolls and doll heads and ordered what they liked and what was inexpensive. One of the biggest, most likely the largest, in the importing trade was George Borgfeldt and it is important that his name especially be mentioned and emphasized. Supposedly he was the first person to come upon the idea of displaying and selling the best and loveliest European dolls made of porcelain, cloth, metal, celluloid and composition in New York. The lovely dolls with bisque heads which were produced in Germany were among these and inspired large orders, so Borgfeldt deserves to be honored and praised for what he did for the German doll industry. Borgfeldt's own great career was made with the dolls. His career began in 1865 as a salesman in New York. Around 1881, he started his business, George Borgfeldt & Co. and very soon he opened branch offices in Europe and Canada. Before World War I he owned the sole sales rights in America and Canada for the dolls of Kämmer & Reinhardt, Kestner, Handwerck and others. The K & K Toy Company was also owned by him. Prominent designers, for example, Joseph L. Kallus, Rose O'Neill, Grace Drayton, Jeno Juszko, Grace Storey Putnam, Georgene Averill, Helen Jensen and others had worked for him, and we have to thank him as well as for the creation of such lovely baby dolls.

Many of the dolls and doll heads chosen by the buyers were also sold in Germany and exported to other countries. Beyond all this, the German porcelain factories also received order for making very special models which were either designed in America or made from special specifications. Wishes such as designs for a laughing baby approximately one year old with a wig or for a crying baby three months old with molded hair, and so forth, were made. In both of these instances, designers or sculptors were hired to produce the designs. Once the designs were approved and all the prerequisites were fulfilled, models were made from which the doll heads would later be produced. These could then be manufactured in various countries and in different materials such as composition, celluloid, wood or cloth. However, if they were to be produced in bisque, they were made in Germany because the porcelain factories there were specialized and could offer both high quality and a good price. After completion, these dolls or doll heads were then sent to America and were seldom sold in Germany. That is why they are relatively unknown there, although in time they were bought back by German collectors.

The most famous example of such a special model was the *Bye-Lo Baby*, also called the *Million Dollar Baby*. This story is worth telling: Grace Putnam was a highly gifted sculptor and designer. In the 1920s she worked as an art teacher at Mills College, Oakland, California. She lived under modest conditions and her biggest wish was to realize one of her designs and become successful and wealthy. When her two

Copr. by Grace S. Putnam MADE IN GERMANY

Neck mark of a *Bye-Lo Baby*.

Minnit Baby from Armand Marseille in an old cloth dress with lace and hand-stitched border (also see page 75).

children were still small, she had made several simple dolls for them which found immediate praise and acknowledgement amongst her friends. She was often requested to produce dolls after her own designs and to sell them. This thought kept her occupied and would not leave her alone. She came upon the idea of modeling a newborn baby, since she often had observed that it was the helplessness of a newborn which stirred the hearts of both adults and children. She searched in various hospitals until she found a newborn infant which fulfilled her ideas.

This happened approximately 11 years after the appearance of the *Kaiser Baby* from Kämmer & Reinhardt. After it, many baby dolls were made by all the doll manufacturers and in many versions. Naturally, in the meantime, one had distanced oneself from these realistic babies because they were found not to be pretty enough and therefore, between 1910 and 1920 one produced more of the toddler-age small children with smooth, sweet doll faces, mostly with sleep eyes and wigs. So it happened that this idea of a baby doll, which in the meantime had become slightly outdated, was once more revived by Grace Putnam for America. She created a very realistic and expressive bust of a three-day-old child. The first model was made out of clay in the hospital. From it a plaster cast was formed and then a wax imprint was taken and the newborn infant was created.

At first it seemed that she would never be able to sell her model. It had taken some time before the idea of offering this model to George Borgfeldt came to her. This baby head pleased him so much that he decided to take it up in his program. They sold rather slowly at first but during the Christmas of 1924, the sales rose to an unbelievable height. That is why it was stated: "Millions of dolls were sold and millions of dollars were earned," earning it the new name, the "Million-Dollar-Baby."

This *Bye-Lo* was produced in various versions, the first ones in wax. The German companies Alt, Beck & Gottschalk, Hertel, Schwab & Co., Kestner and Kiling & Co., took over the production of the heads and small *Bye-Los* in bisque. Cameo Doll Co., in New York produced the composition heads. The celluloid heads were produced by Karl Standfuss, a celluloid doll factory in Deuben near Dresden, and wooden heads were manufactured by Schoenhut in Philadelphia. The *Bye-Lo* baby was available with various colored skin, with painted or with glass sleep eyes. The bodies were initially made of composition but shortly afterwards, they were mainly made of cloth and were designed by Georgene Averill. The beautiful well-formed hands were mostly made of celluloid or composition. The sizes varied between 3⅛in (8cm) up to the life-sized 10⅝in (50cm). For nearly three years the *Bye-Lo* was the best selling baby doll in America and because of this, Grace Putnam became a very wealthy woman. She worked for some time as a designer for Borgfeldt and designed among other dolls the *Crying Bye-Lo* (see page 34, left) and *Fly-Lo*.

The *Crying Bye-Lo* was a delicate, smoother version of the baby *Bye-Lo* with turned down corners of the mouth as if it would start to cry, and with molded-on glass tears already rolling down the cheeks. The *Fly-Lo* is an independent and completely different type of baby. Grace Putnam was thinking more of a doll fairy with wings, which did not agree, however, with the ideas of George Borgfeldt who was expecting another baby doll. Naturally, he wanted to repeat the success of the *Bye-Lo* baby. So two years after the *Bye-Lo* baby, the *Fly-Lo*, a small baby doll with glass eyes, whose original clothing was supposedly a pink-colored silk costume with cape and wings, was produced. It was not born for success because an economic crisis had arisen. The import/export business had problems, causing the production of the *Fly-Lo* to be halted after only a few were produced.

In the meantime, the *Bye-Lo* baby had become well-known in Germany, but there were a number of beautiful baby dolls which are relatively unknown in Germany. We would like to introduce a small selection of these dolls which were rather popular in America. Since it was impossible for us, even after an enormous effort, to get original photographs of all of these, it was decided to introduce our readers to reproductions of these (see pages 100-103).

A small baby doll from Swaine & Co. Neck mark: "F.P.I." (green markings) "S & C geschutz Germany." Socket head, open-closed mouth, bent-limb baby body, 11¹/₈in (28cm).

TO ALL CAPTIONS
In this book, nearly all baby dolls that we show have mainly bisque heads and most of these bodies are made of composition. Exceptions are clearly noted. Those musical names, for example Hilda, Butterfly Baby *or* Mein Lieblings Baby (My Favorite Baby) *are mainly registered tradenames; some have fantasy names — for example, the name* Kaiser Baby.

Alt, Beck & Gottschalk, the first character baby of this company. Neck Mark: "A. B. & G. 1319." Socket head, painted hair, light blue painted eyes, toddler body with ten joints, 11⁷/₈in (30cm), circa 1910.

Right-handside baby like above, left-handside baby from Bruno Schmidt (also see page 80).

Far right page: Baehr & Proeschild. Neck mark: "BP" (in a heart) "585 11 made in Germany." Socket head, mohair wig, blue sleep eyes, open mouth with two upper teeth, toddler body with ten joints, 21⁵/₈in (55cm), circa 1915, old clothing.

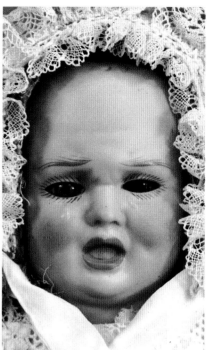

Carl Bergner, Sonneberg. A very rare doll with three faces, marked on the back of the breast plate: "C. B." (in a circle). Socket head on shoulder plate (breast plate), head with three faces, crown of the head with knob to turn, blue fixed glass eyes, cloth body with arms and legs of composition, 11⁷/₈in (30cm).

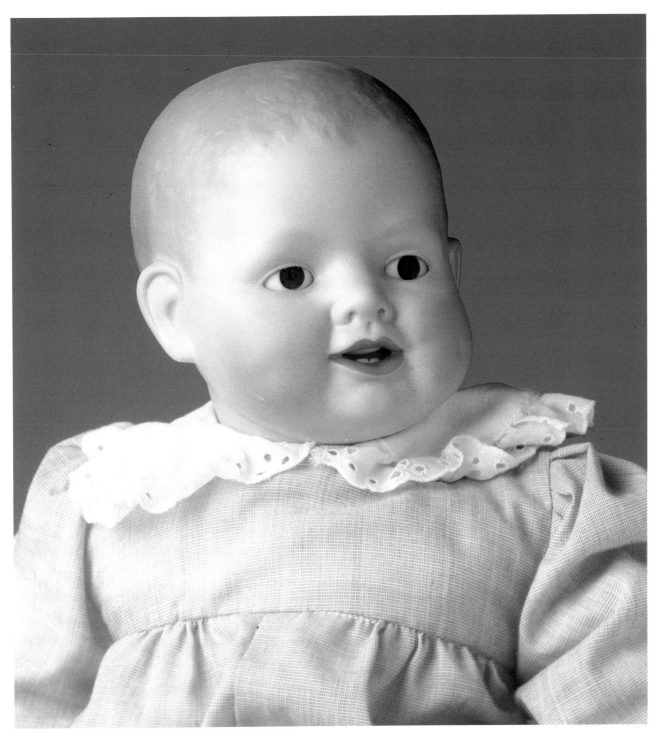

Bonnie Babe, the (one-year-old) baby doll from Georgene Averill. Neck mark: "Copr. by Georgene Averill 1005/3652/4 Germany." Producer: Alt, Beck & Gottschalk for Georgene Averill. Flange neck head, molded and painted hair, open mouth with two upper teeth, brown fixed glass eyes, cloth body with arms and legs of composition, $20^7/s$in (53cm), circa 1925.

The *Crying Bye-Lo* is a version of the *Bye-Lo Baby*. Flange neck head with molded and painted hair, brown glass eyes and molded tears, closed mouth with turned down corners, cloth body, 11⁷/₈in (30cm). Reproduction: Christel Kesting, 1986. Right picture: The *Bye-Lo* with original clothes including bonnet.

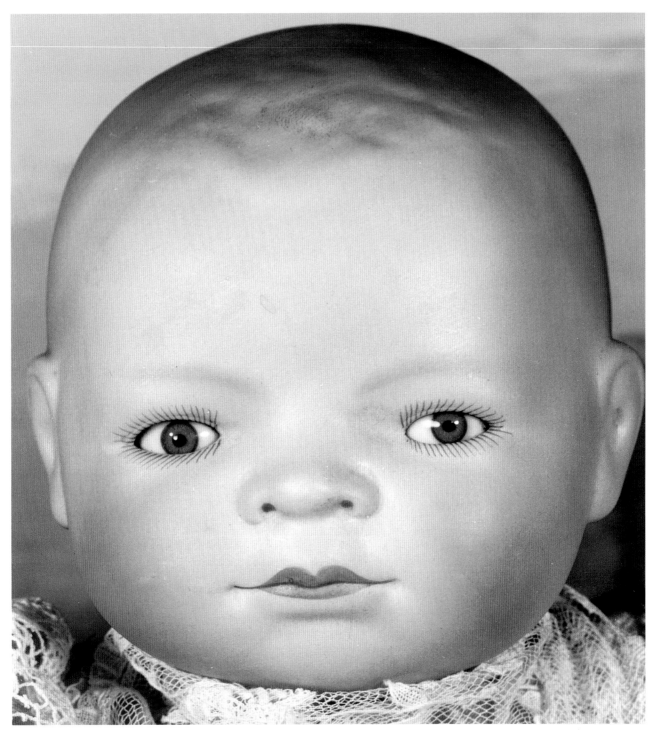

Bye-Lo Baby, the (three-day-old) baby doll. Neck mark: "Copr. by Grace S. Putnam, made in Germany." Producer: Kestner for George Borgfeldt, New York. Flange neck head, molded and painted hair, closed mouth, cloth body (see page 24, bottom row middle), celluloid hands, 17³/₄in (45cm), circa 1925.

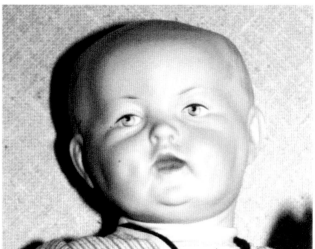

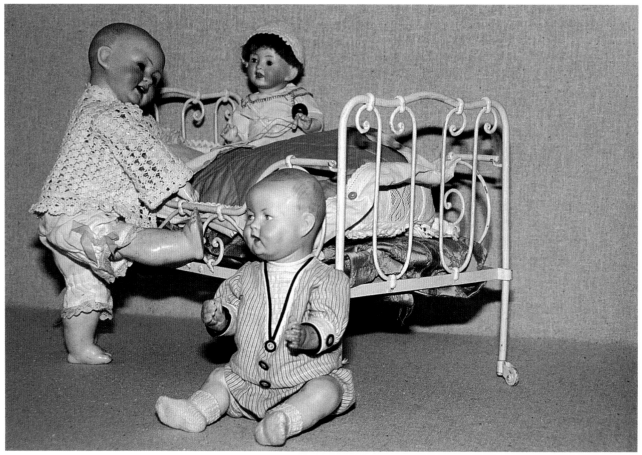

Catterfelder Doll Factory
Above left: Neck mark: "C.P. 208/34 deponiert." Socket head, painted eyes, open-closed mouth with two molded upper teeth, bent-limb baby body, 13³/₄in (35cm), circa 1912.

Above right: Neck mark: "C.P. 201." Socket head, painted eyes, open-closed mouth, bent-limb baby body, 11⁷/₈in (30cm), circa 1912.
Below: Left doll: neck mark: "C.P. 208/34" with glass eyes. The doll in bed: neck mark: "C.P. 208/28," with wig.

Cuno & Otto Dressel. Neck mark: "1920/11
Jutta-Baby Dressel 10." Socket head, open
mouth with two upper teeth, flirting eyes,
baby body with movable hand joints, 18⁷/₈in
(48cm), — circa 1920. Doll head made by
Simon & Halbig.

F. & W. Goebel. Neck mark: (crown WG) "B 5 - 8½ Germany." Socket head, blonde mohair wig, glass sleep eyes, open mouth with two upper teeth, bent-limb baby body, 18⅛in (46cm), circa 1915.

Heinrich Handwerck. Socket head, blue glass sleep eyes, open mouth with two upper teeth, brown mohair wig, toddler body with ten joints, 17¾in (45cm), circa 1910.

Kewpie (left): all-bisque, 9in (23cm), designed by Rose O'Neill, produced by Kestner for Borgfeldt, 1914.
Unmarked baby doll (right): all-bisque, 6¾in (16cm).

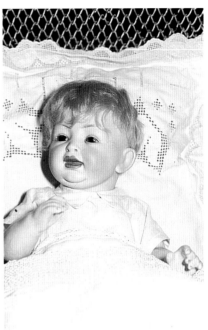

Presumably Hertel, Schwab & Co. Neck mark "150/4." Socket head, brown glass sleep eyes, open-closed mouth, light-blonde mohair wig, bent-limb baby body, 12⅝in (32cm), circa 1915.

Presumably Hertel, Schwab & Co. for Louis Wolf and Co., New York. Neck mark: "152." Socket head, open mouth with four upper teeth and molded-on tongue, mohair wig, toddler body with ten joints, 19⅝in (50cm), circa 1915.

Ernst Heubach, Köppelsdorf. Neck mark:
"Heubach-Koppelsdorf 320-2½ Germany."
Mulatto: socket head baby, brown sleep eyes,
open mouth with two upper teeth, original
mohair wig, brown baby body, 17³/₈in (44cm),
circa 1920.

Ernst Heubach, Koppelsdorf: Southsea baby
produced for A. Luge & Co., Sonneberg.
Neck mark: "Heubach Koppelsdorf
D.R.G.M. Germany ³⁹⁹/₇/9." Socket head,
dark brown sleep eyes, dark brown baby
body, 11½in (29cm).

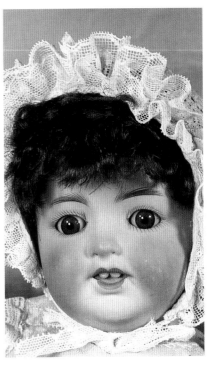

Ernst Heubach, Köppelsdorf. Neck mark: "342/3 Germany II." Blue-gray glass sleep eyes, open mouth with two large upper teeth, baby body.

Ernst Heubach, Köppelsdorf. Neck mark: "Heubach Koppelsdorf 339-3/0 Germany." Flange neck head, closed mouth, sleep eyes, cloth body, celluloid hands, 15³/₄in (40cm), circa 1925. Also produced as a black doll or as an Oriental.

Left: Gebr. Heubach: baby number 339, like above.
Right: Unmarked baby, socket head, closed mouth, 13³/₄in (35cm).

Gebr. Heubach: small *Baby Stuart*. Neck mark: "79 77 (Heubach sun)." Socket head with molded on bonnet, blue intaglio eyes, bent-limb baby body, no painted eye lashes but reddish painted eyeliner, 7¹/₂in (19cm), circa 1912.

Gebr. Heubach: an unusually large and beautiful *Baby Stuart*. Neck mark: "79 77 (Heubach sun)." Socket head with molded on bonnet, painted blue intaglio eyes, bent-limb baby body, no painted eye lashes but reddish eyeliner, 18⅞in (48cm), circa 1915, old clothing.

◀ Gebr. Heubach, Lichte. Neck mark: "0,6914 Germany." Socket head, molded hair, blue intaglio eyes, closed mouth, bent-limb baby body, 7⁷/₈in (20cm), circa 1915.

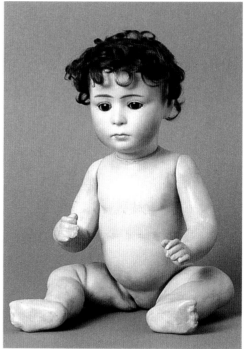

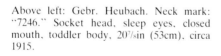

Above left: Gebr. Heubach. Neck mark: "7246." Socket head, sleep eyes, closed mouth, toddler body, 20⅞in (53cm), circa 1915.

Below left: Gebr. Heubach: *Baby Stuart* with Teddy Bear. Wearing an old long dress, 18⅞in (48cm).
Above and below right: see page 45.

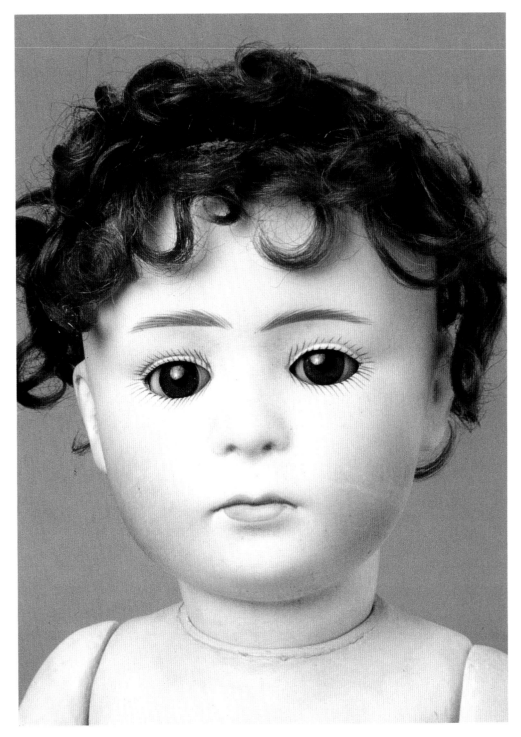

Gebr. Heubach. Neck mark: "7246-5 Germany (Heubach sun)." Socket head, brown sleep eyes, closed mouth, original mohair wig, bent-limb baby body, 13in (33cm), circa 1915, old clothing.

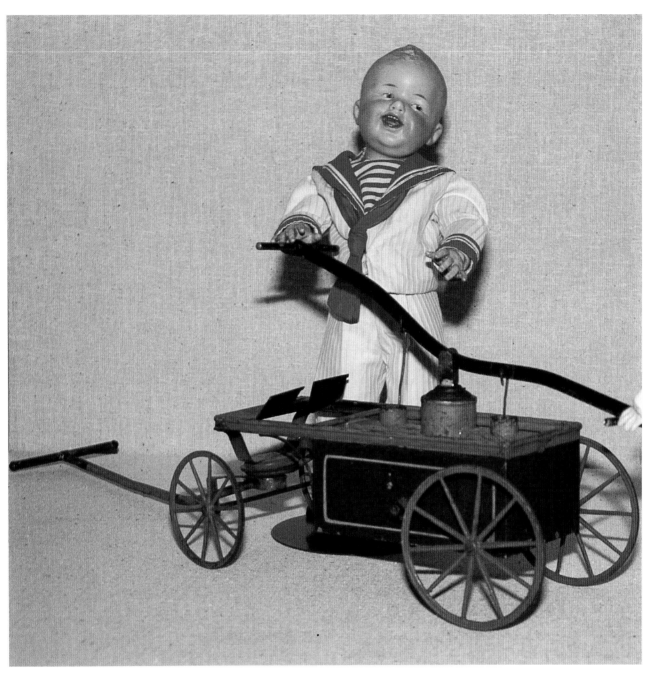

Left page, above left: Gebr. Heubach. Neck mark: "3 Germany." Shoulder head, intaglio eyes, open-closed mouth with two molded lower teeth (so-called shark teeth), mohair wig, leather body, 13¾in (35cm), circa 1915.

Left page, above right: Gebr. Heubach. Neck mark: "7634." Socket bald head, open-closed mouth with molded tongue, intaglio eyes, bent-limb baby body, 8⅞in (22cm).

Left page, bottom left and right: Very rare mechanical twins from Gebr. Heubach. Heads with molded on hair, dark blue painted eyes, open-closed mouth with two lower teeth, 10¼in (26cm). Carrying cushion covered in silk and decorated with lace, ruffles and bows, including a music box (when one squeezes the cushion with both thumbs, the music starts and both heads of the dolls turn sideways). Most likely the heads are similar to that of the above left-hand picture.

Gebr. Heubach. Neck mark: "Heubach" (in a square) "8191 Germany." Socket head with molded-on hair, intaglio eyes, laughing open-closed mouth with four upper and two lower molded teeth, toddler body with ten joints, 13¾in (35cm), circa 1912, original clothing, old fire-wagon.

Gebr. Heubach: a very special expressive, amusing and rare character child. Neckmark: "8588 Heubach" (in a square "18"(?), socket head gray-blue intaglio eyes, closed pouting mouth, mohair wig, straight-leg baby body, 13³/₈in (34cm), circa 1920. This same model head is also available with a bald head and molded hair, marked with the number 8548.

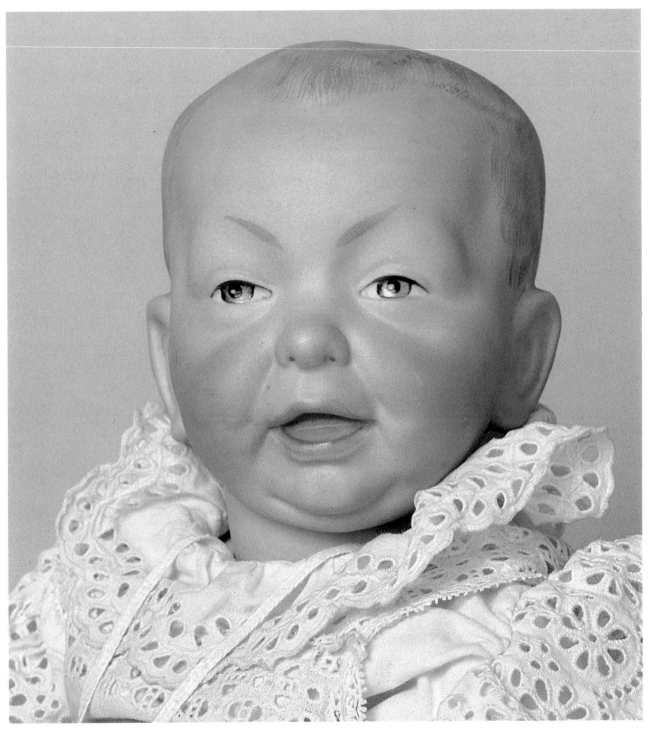

The first realistic baby doll from Kämmer & Reinhardt, the so-called (*Kaiser Baby*). Neck mark: "K" (a star) "R 100/36." Socket head with slightly molded and painted hair, painted blue eyes, open-closed mouth bent-limb baby body with four joints, 14^{1}/$_{8}$in (36cm), circa 1909, old clothing. The *Kaiser Baby* was available in four versions: with glass eyes, open dome-head with wig, as a black doll or as an Oriental.

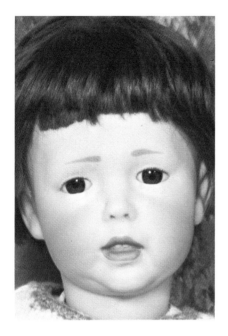

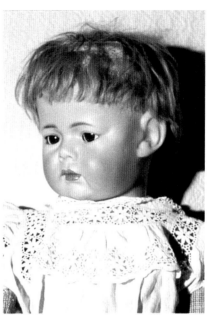

Neck mark: "K" (a star) "R 112.43." Socket head, open-closed mouth with two upper teeth, glass eyes, bent-limb baby body, 13³/₈in (34cm). Also produced with painted eyes.

Neck mark: "K" (a star) "R 119 Baby." Same mold as that of 115A. Socket head, closed mouth, glass sleep eyes, toddler body with ten joints, 26³/₄in (68cm), circa 1915.

Neck mark: "K" (a star) "R 122." Socket head, glass sleep eyes, open mouth with two upper teeth, bent-limb baby body, 8⁵/₈in (22cm), circa 1915.

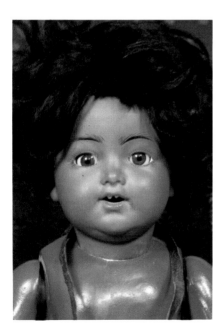

Neck mark: "K" (a star) "R Simon & Halbig 126." Socket head made from brown tinted bisque, open mouth with two upper teeth, original black wig, brown bent-limb baby body, circa 1915.

Neck mark: "K" (a star) "R Simon & Halbig ¹²⁷/₂₆." Socket head, blue glass sleep eyes, open mouth with two molded glass upper teeth, molded and painted hair, bent-limb baby body, 10¹/₄in (26cm), circa 1915, old clothing.

Neck mark: "K" (a star) "R 128." Socket head, sleep eyes, open mouth, bent-limb baby body with four joints, 18⁷/₈in (48cm), circa 1915.

The small doll is marked with a number 122 (see left page, top row right).

This large doll has a neck mark: "K" (a star) "R Simon & Halbig 121." Socket head, blue glass sleep eyes, blonde mohair wig, open mouth with two upper teeth and a separate tongue, toddler body with ten joints, 23⁵/₈in (60cm), circa 1915, old clothing.

Kämmer & Reinhardt. Neck mark: 127
Simon & Halbig - 26.'' Socket head, molded
and painted hair, blue glass sleep eyes, open
mouth with two upper glass teeth, bent-limb
baby body with four joints, 10¼in (26cm),
circa 1915, old clothing.

Kämmer & Reinhardt. Neck mark: "K" (a star) "R Simon & Halbig 126." Socket head, old human hair wig, blue glass sleep eyes, open mouth with two upper teeth and a molded tongue, baby body with four joints, circa 1915, original clothing, (see page 96, bottom picture). *My Favorite Baby* was made with all composition body types, in white or colored, with flirty eyes, with the eye mechanism (Der Unart) (naughty) with a mamma or pappa voice.

Kämmer & Reinhardt. Neck mark: "K" (a star) "R Simon & Halbig 116/A 32." Socket head, left doll blue and right doll brown sleep eyes, both with open-closed mouth with two molded upper teeth, old mohair wigs, both toddler bodies (right body in brown), both 15in (38cm), circa 1915. This doll was also made with painted hair and the number 116 doll was made with open mouth, two upper teeth and movable tongue. Above dolls with bent-limb baby bodies were 12⅝in (32cm).

Kämmer & Reinhardt. Neck mark: "K" (a star) "R 118." Very rare, socket head, old human hair wig, blue glass sleep eyes, open mouth with two upper teeth, two large dimples in the cheek and one in the chin, toddler body, 18⅞in (48cm), circa 1915, old clothing.

J.D. Kestner (most likely). No neck mark. Socket head, molded and painted hair, painted blue eyes, open-closed mouth, bent-limb baby body, 13¾in (35cm), circa 1915, old clothing. Since this doll head has neither neck mark nor the usual Kestner baby body, one suspects that this doll was made for one or more companies.

J.D. Kestner. Neck mark: "JDK 12." Unusually rare and beautiful baby doll. Socket head with molded-on blue and white bonnet with porcelain lace, molded and painted blonde curls, open mouth with two upper teeth, baby body, 15in (38cm), circa 1915, an old nightdress. Photograph: *Auction house Christie's, London.*

J.D. Kestner. Neck mark: "178." All-bisque, socket head, blue glass sleep eyes, brown fur wig, open-closed mouth with two lower molded teeth, straight-leg baby body, 8$\frac{1}{4}$in (21cm).

J.D. Kestner. Neck mark: "H made in Germany $\frac{12}{211}$ JDK." Socket head, old blonde mohair wig, blue glass sleep eyes, open mouth with two lower teeth, bent-limb baby body, 15$\frac{3}{4}$in (40cm), circa 1915.

J.D. Kestner. Neck mark: "Made in Germany J.D.K. 226." Socket head, blue glass sleep eyes, open mouth with two upper teeth and molded tongue, old blonde mohair wig, bent-limb baby body, old baptismal dress with lace, 15$\frac{3}{4}$in (40cm), circa 1915.

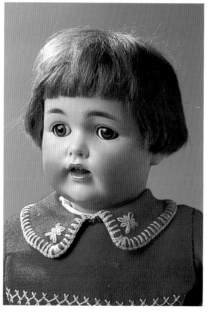

J.D. Kestner. Neck mark: "Made in Germany J.D.K. 257." Socket head, blonde mohair wig, brown glass sleep eyes, open mouth with two upper teeth, bent-limb baby body, 16$\frac{1}{4}$in (41cm), made after 1914.

J.D. Kestner. Neck mark: "J.D.K. 260 made in Germany G 57." Socket head, blue flirty eyes, open mouth with upper teeth, toddler body, 25$\frac{5}{8}$in (65cm), circa 1915, old rose-colored dress with embroidery.

J.D. Kestner: *Hilda.* One of the most beloved and sought-after baby dolls. Neck mark: "J.D.K. Jr. 1914 ges. -gesch. N 1070 made in Germany." Socket bald head with painted hair, bent-limb baby body, 23$\frac{1}{4}$in (59cm).

J.D. Kestner: *Hilda.* Neck mark: "Made in Germany M¹⁶/₂₃₇ JDK Jr. 1914 Hilda ges. gesch. N 1070." Socket head, original mohair wig, brown glass sleep eyes, open mouth with two upper teeth and a molded tongue, baby body, 23¼in (59cm), circa 1914, original condition.

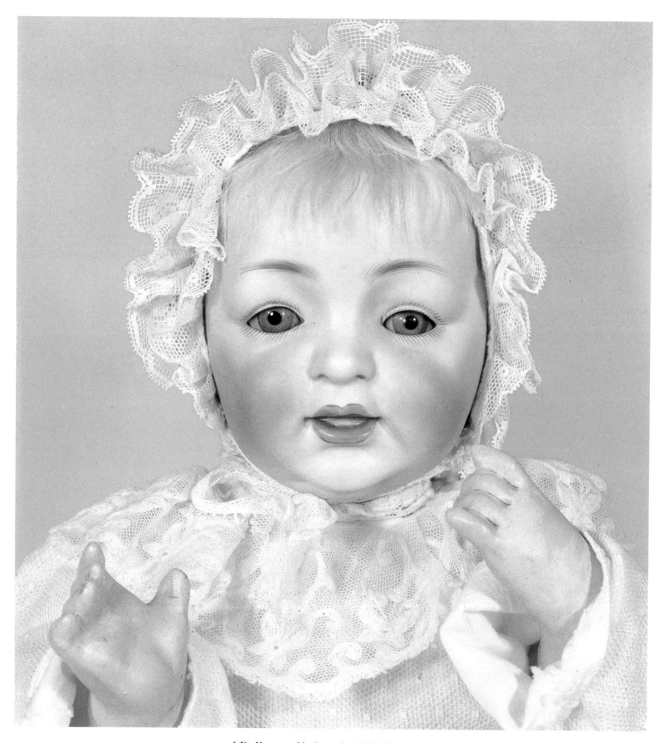

J.D. Kestner. Neck mark: "J.D.K. made in Germany 211." Socket head with original plaster dome top, blue glass sleep eyes, open-closed mouth with molded gums and two teeth, body (see page 24, top row, middle), 16½in (42cm), circa 1915.

J.D. Kestner. Neck mark: "JDK 235." Shoulder head with original closed plaster dome, old blonde mohair wig, sleep eyes, open mouth with two lower teeth, rare leather body with Kestner crown, 13³/₄in (35cm), circa 1915.

J.D. Kestner for Century Doll Co. Neck mark: CENTURY DOLL CO., Kestner." Socket head, slightly molded and painted hair, glass sleep eyes, closed mouth, bent-limb baby body, baby voice-box, 10¼in (26cm), circa 1925.

Large picture above and top left: J.D. Kestner. Neck mark: "JDK made in Germany 243." Oriental, yellow tinted socket head, open mouth with two upper teeth and tongue, brown sleep eyes, bent-limb baby body, 13¾in (35cm), circa 1915, original clothing.

A small unmarked boy doll, most likely made by Kley & Hahn.

Kley & Hahn. Neck mark: "K & H made in Germany." Socket head, original mohair wig, sleep eyes, open mouth with two upper teeth and tongue, bent-limb baby body, 18⁷/₈in (48cm), circa 1918.

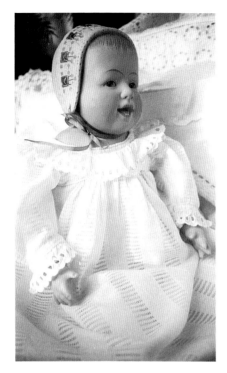

Top picture: This doll is wearing old baby clothing (side view of the finely painted bonnet).
Below: Rear view of molded bisque bonnet.

Gebr. Knoch, Coburg. Neck mark: "Made in Germany Ge. Nr. 233 Gesch." Beautiful and rare shoulder head with molded and painted bonnet. The bonnet has a hole on each side so that a ribbon can be threaded through and tied. Molded and painted hair, blue intaglio eyes, open-closed mouth with molded tongue and two lower teeth, cloth body, 15³/₄in (40cm), circa 1920.

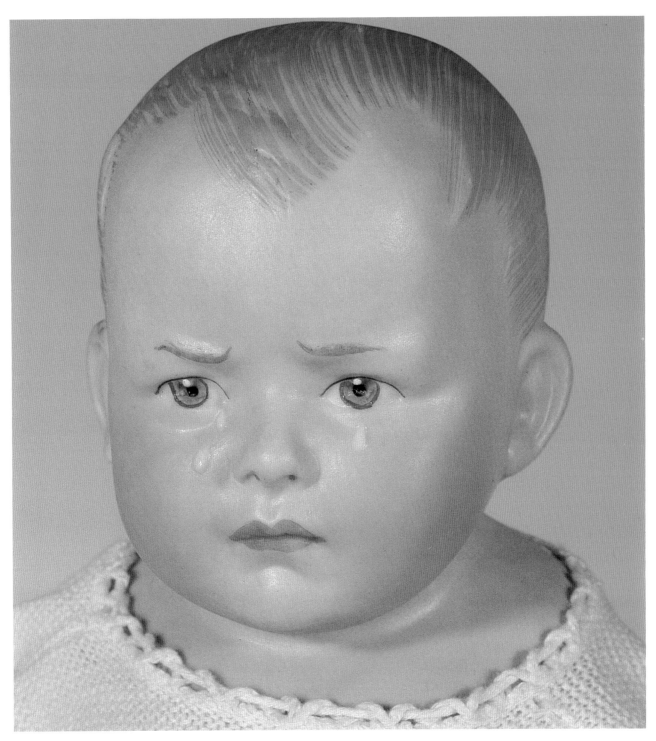

Gebr. Knoch. Unusual strong character, lovely and rare baby doll. Marking on shoulder plate: "G.K." (two crossed bones) "N. made in Germany Ges. N. 223 Gesch. G/o." Shoulder head: height 4³/₄in (12cm), width 4¹/₄in (11cm). Crying expressive face with molded-on tears, molded and painted hair, pouting closed mouth, bulging eyebrows, circa 1915. A leather baby body belongs to this head.

Koenig & Wernicke. The head is most likely produced by Hertel, Schwab & Co. Neck mark: "98 made in Germany." Socket head, blue sleep eyes, open mouth, bent-limb baby body, 15¾in (40cm), circa 1915.

Koenig & Wernicke: sweet *Butterfly Baby*. The head is most likely produced by Hertel, Schwab & Co., not to be confused with the *Butterfly Baby* produced by Kestner for Horsman. Neck mark: "Butterfly Baby 90/3/o made in Germany." Socket head, brown glass eyes, open-closed mouth with molded oral cavity, molded-on tongue with two separate upper teeth, standing baby body with round stamp from Koenig & Wernicke, 13in (33cm).

The *Dream Baby* without fluffy hair.

Armand Marseille: the so-called *Crying Dream Baby*. Neck mark: "A.M. Germany 342/0." Flange neck head, glass sleep eyes, open-closed mouth, cloth body, forearm and legs made of composition, 11in (28cm), circa 1925.

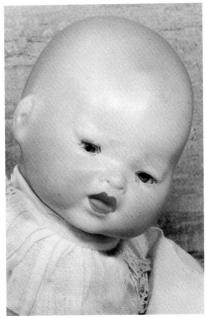

◄ Marseille, Armand: *My Dream Baby* is being taken for a walk by a large doll from Simon & Halbig.

Large picture: Armand Marseille: *My Dream Baby*. Neck mark: "AM 341 6K." Socket head, molded and painted hair as well as glued-on fluffy hair, blue sleep eyes, closed mouth, bent-limb baby body, 17³/₄in (45cm), circa 1925, old child's clothing, knitted of fine cotton yarn and embroidered with beads. This *Dream Baby* was also available with an open mouth and two teeth, and had a neck mark "351" and with "620" in all-bisque.

Marseille, Armand: *My Dream Baby*, black version.

◄ Armand Marseille: *My Dream Baby* as a black baby. Neck mark: "A.M. Germany, 341/3." Flange neck head, brown glass sleep eyes, closed mouth, cloth baby body with hands made of composition, mamma voice, 11¾in (30cm), circa 1925.

▲ Armand Marseille: *My Dream Baby* as an Oriental. Neck mark: "A.M. Ellar" (in a star) "Germany 2 K." Dark brown sleep eyes, yellow tinted socket head, closed mouth, yellow tinted bent-limb baby body, 11¾in (30cm), circa 1926, clothing made of old China silk.

71

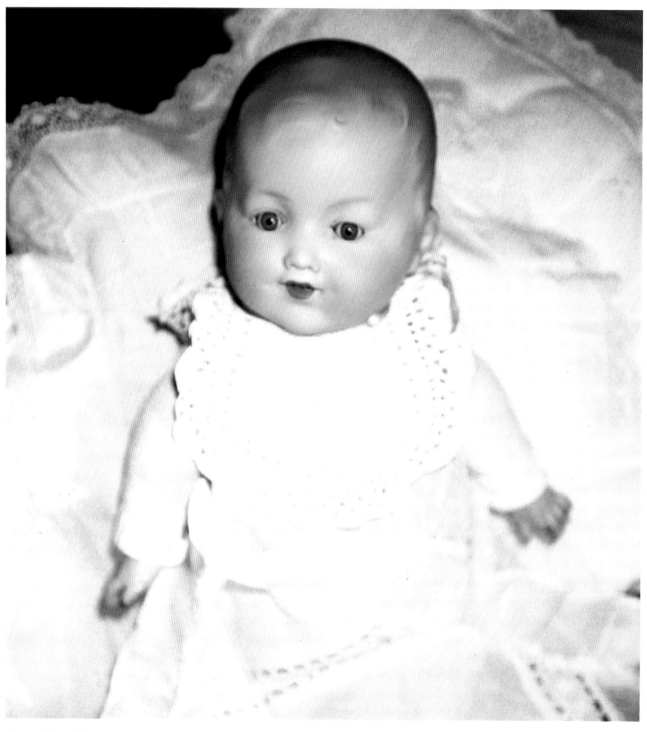

Armand Marseille. *Baby Love* produced for America. Neck mark: "A.M. 352 Germany." Flange neck head, molded and painted hair, blue sleep eyes, open mouth with two upper teeth, cloth body with hands made of composition, 15¾in (40cm), circa 1920, old baptismal dress with crocheted bib.

Armand Marseille, Neck mark: "AM 700 ⁴/₀." Socket head, blue sleep eyes, old mohair wig, closed pouty mouth, bent-limb baby body with four joints, 9³/₄in (25cm), circa 1918, old doll's clothing, an especially sweet doll.

Armand Marseille: *Fany*. Socket head, light
blue sleep eyes, original mohair wig, closed
mouth, toddler body with eight joints, 13³/₄in
(35cm), circa 1915.

Armand Marseille. Both babies were produced for America.
Left: *Minnit Baby* for George Borgfeldt. Neck mark: "971 A. 5 M. D.R.G.M. 267/in Germany." Socket head, blue sleep eyes, open mouth with two upper teeth, toddler body, 18¹/sin (46cm), circa 1912.
Right: *Dorothy*. Neck mark: "Made in Germany A. 2.M. 560 a D.R.M.R. 232." Socket head, blue sleep eyes, open mouth with two upper teeth, toddler body with ten joints, 15in (38cm), circa 1915.

Porcelain Factory Mengersgereuth. Neck
mark: "P.M. 914." Socket head, brown sleep
eyes, old mohair wig, open mouth with six
upper teeth and molded-on tongue, bent-limb
baby body with four joints, 19⅝in (50cm),
circa 1920.

Theodor Recknagel. Neck mark: "Germany
6 R 141 A." Socket head with painted hair,
sleep eyes, closed mouth, type (newborn),
21⁵/₈in (55cm), circa 1920, old baby clothing.

Tube mechanism of the crying baby doll from Hertel, Schwab & Co.

Hertel, Schwab & Co. for Schachner: crying character doll. Neck mark: "148 6." Fixed blue glass eyes, open-closed mouth, original blonde mohair wig, baby body with bent arms and legs, 15³/₄in (40cm), circa 1915, original clothing. In the head of the doll there is an apparatus to which a thin tube is connected to a small hand pump, which is filled with water. By depressing this pump, little tears trickle out of the eyes.

Not only in the profile (left picture) but also from the front does Bruno Schmidt's *Wendy* look like a beautiful doll.

Bruno Schmidt. Neck mark: "2033 BSW" (in a heart) "537." Human hair wig, blue sleep eyes, closed mouth, bent-limb baby body 15in (38cm), circa 1915. Very strong expressive profile of an unusually beautiful doll.

The same doll as right, but only with a wig.

Bruno Schmidt. Neck mark: "2024/4/540/6." The head is presumably made by Baehr & Proeschild. A very rare and beautiful baby. Socket bald head, painted hair painted blue eyes with red eyeliner, closed mouth, bent-limb baby body with four joints, 14¼in (36cm), circa 1915, wearing an old dress.

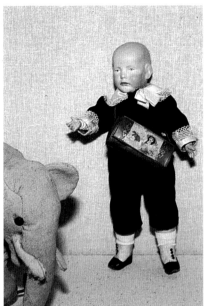

Franz Schmidt. Neck mark: "F.S & Co. 1267." Socket head, painted blue eyes, closed mouth, toddler body, 13¾in (35cm), circa 1915, old clothing.

Franz Schmidt. Neck mark: "F.S & C 1272/35Z Deponiert." Socket bald head with molded and painted hair, light blue sleep eyes, open mouth with two upper teeth and molded tongue, toddler body, 14½in (37cm), circa 1915, copied clothing made from old material.

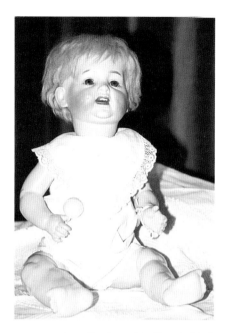

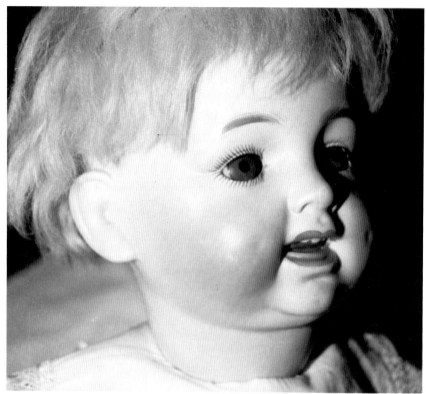

Schoenau & Hoffmeister: *My Cherub*. Neck mark: "MB" (in a circle). Socket head, old mohair wig, sleep eyes, open mouth, bent-limb baby body, 19⁵/₈in (50cm), circa 1920, old clothing.

Schoenau & Hoffmeister: *Hanna*. Neck mark: "SPB" (in a star) "H Hanna." Socket head, sleep eyes, open mouth with two upper teeth, bent-limb baby body, circa 1920. *Hanna* was also available as an Oriental or as a Polynesian.

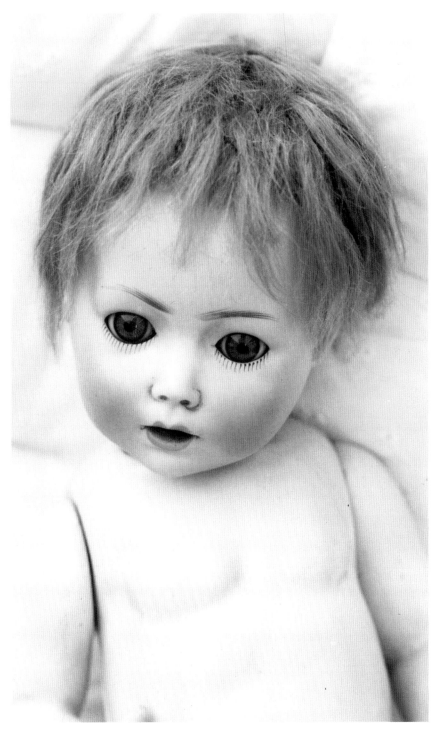

The same baby but with a bonnet and a long nightgown.

Schoenau & Hoffmeister. Neck mark: "SPB" (in a star) "H." Socket head, blonde mohair wig, blue sleep eyes, open mouth, bent-limb baby body, 13in (33cm), circa 1920.

Simon & Halbig. Neck mark: "1488 Simon & Halbig." Socket head, original human hair wig, blue glass sleep eyes, open-closed mouth, toddler body with ten joints, 30½in (80cm), circa 1915. A very beautiful and rare baby doll.

Simon & Halbig: a very lovely and sought after baby doll. Neck mark: "Erika Simon & Halbig 1489." Blue sleep eyes, open mouth with two upper teeth and a tongue, bent-limb baby body 23⁵/₈in (60cm), circa 1918, old baby clothing.

Simon & Halbig: named *Freddy*. Neck mark: "1428." Socket head, strong featured face with small swellings around the eyes, small sleep eyes, open-closed mouth with molded tongue, a strong double chin, bent-limb baby body, 13¾in (35cm), made in 1915.

Simon & Halbig. A very rare and expressive baby doll. Neck mark: "1498 Simon & Halbig. Socket bald head with painted hair, gray-blue sleep eyes, open-closed mouth, toddler body, 22³/₄in (58cm), made around 1918, very lovely old clothing.

A very charming old doll buggy made in France.

Société Française de Fabrication de Bébés of Jouets (S.F.B.J.)

To report about French baby dolls means essentially to write about the babies of S.F.B.J. (the French doll and toy society corporation). Other French manufacturers of porcelain doll heads had, as far as is known, not produced any babies, whereby baby dolls made of celluloid and other materials were not considered. After the founding of S.F.B.J. in April of 1899, there were no other companies worth mentioning next to this mighty corporation. Jumeau, Gaultier, Girard (Bru) and Fleischmann & Bloedel belonged to S.F.B.J., other companies slowly disappearing one by one, as did Steiner around 1907.

At first the shareholders of S.F.B.J. had problems in addition to the development of new doll types. The material bought from the other companies had to be sifted. The majority of all the doll parts and apparatus came from Jumeau, a company which produced large amounts until it shut down. Their *Bébé Jumeau* (not a baby, but a girl of 12 years of age) had become well-known throughout the world. There was no question that this bébé would continue to be produced. The same thing happened to *Bébé Bru* and its sister, *Bébé Têteur*, which since 1879 continued to be sold with an unchanged face, but now with a Jumeau body. Of the many other well-known babies, only the successful models continued to be produced for a short time, for example, the *Eden Bébé*.

The success of the German baby dolls were not hidden from the French doll industry, S.F.B.J. soon followed suit. Their first character doll was the number 226. This baby with a bald head, open-closed mouth and glass eyes resembled the *Kaiser Baby* (K & R 100) rather strongly; it was definitely copied. A special baby body was developed with bent arms and legs, anatomically well designed and of outstanding sitting ability. A lovely detail was its large spread big toes.

Since the head of the doll number 226 was rather child-like, but not baby-like, it was used on the well-known jointed body as well as on the less expensive half-jointed body and became a boy doll. The same method was used with several later models, with only a few of the later and rarer heads being exclusively made for the baby. Very soon a toddler body was made, which in quality and shape was a perfect jointed body of a small child who could already walk. With these few body types, S.F.B.J. could make a baby or a small child, either a boy or a girl of all ages without ever using a new model. The following mold numbers correspond with this pattern:

S.F.B.J. number 227: This number is of a laughing child with a bald head, an open mouth with a set of upper teeth and fixed eyes, in quality very similar to those of the famous paperweight eyes of the French bébés. These eyes, which are to be found with other models (numbers 229, 233, 235, 237 and 238) are very popular among collectors and are called "jewel eyes," due to their depth and glittering effect. The head of doll number 227 has painted hair and is often found on a jointed body, making it a very delightful little boy. It is also available in a black version and in a smaller version with painted eyes on a baby body.

S.F.B.J. number 229: Its expression is very similar to that of number 227; however, it has a far more pronounced smile and a wig. Due to the rather striking double chin, this rather rare doll appears to be more child-like.

S.F.B.J. number 233: This rather rare head of a screaming baby with a bald head, jewel eyes in a very extreme narrow eye socket and an open-closed mouth, belongs to a set of three interchangeable heads (see page 94). The most frequent combinations are the numbers 227, 235 and 237, but also the numbers 233, 227 and 237, whereby the same child could have stood as a model for all of them. The doll with the interchangeable heads could show, depending upon the mood of the playing child, either a friendly, laughing or crying face. Number 233 was also sold as a single doll or sometimes on a baby body.

S.F.B.J. number 234: This number indicates a very rare doll. It has a very child-like face and is mostly found on a baby body. The doll has sleeping eyes, wig and an open mouth with a movable tongue. The model of this child also stood model for the famous number 236.

S.F.B.J. number 235: This is a friendly smiling child with a bald head, fixed eyes and an open-closed mouth with two molded upper teeth. The molded hair was sometimes painted or often sprayed on. A version with painted eyes was also known. This model could be on a baby body, jointed body or a half-jointed body. The quality of the later jointed bodies was rather imperfect.

S.F.B.J. number 236: This lovable, laughing child's face was the biggest success among S.F.B.J.'s character dolls. This head was made for 30 years. It is found mainly on baby bodies and often in larger dolls, also on the toddler bodies favored by collectors. Caution is necessary with all other combinations. The head of the doll number 236 always had sleep eyes and a wig. The smiling open-closed mouth

A very lovely old German painted metal doll buggy.

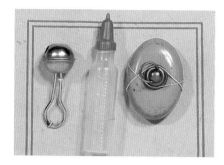

Baby set: hot water bottle 2¹/₈in (6cm), milk bottle 3⁵/₈in (9cm), rattle 2¹/₈in (6cm).

Silver rattles in different sizes between 3in (8cm) and 5¹/₈in (13cm) with bellt, teething rod made of coral and teething ring.

shows two upper teeth, the bottom lip being partially covered by a molded-on tongue. This doll with its dimpled double chin, its full cheeks and the pronounced nose to mouth line is a successful portrait of a well-humored, bright, small child who seems to want to babble his first words. No wonder that it was produced successfully for such a long time and is today loved by so many collectors. The doll number 236 was given a short hair wig with bangs, usually mohair, from blonde to red and in all shades of brown. These original wigs suit the child-like face very well and, therefore, it is unnecessary to disfigure this face with a long hair wig or long curls, quite often seen.

S.F.B.J. numbers 237 and 238: Both heads are very lovely likenesses of an older child. If these heads are found on baby bodies, please be careful! This was not originally planned by the company!

S.F.B.J. number 247: Here a complete new face was created which does not remind one at all of the preceding models. It is a child-like type with a very cute upturned nose, a high, strongly arched forehead and a slight thoughtful expression. This model is well-sought-after by collectors and it is a pity that it does not belong to the more numerous character dolls of S.F.B.J. The doll number 247 has an open-closed mouth, sleep eyes and wig. The body which belongs to this head is either a baby body or a toddler body. Later, this head was made of composition and also a version was produced with compressed felt mounted on a cloth body with straight legs.

S.F.B.J. number 251: This highly individual face had pronounced fat cheeks with dimples, sleep eyes and an open mouth with a movable tongue. This head is mainly found on either a baby or toddler body. From 1925 on, this head, like a few others, was marked with "UNIS FRANCE." When so marked, it is more strongly tinted or is made of composition.

S.F.B.J. number 252: This head belongs to those star dolls of collectors of character dolls. The child-like grumpy face with a tightly closed mouth, the defiant pushed out upper lip and the slightly drooping corners of the mouth does not equal the expression of any other doll! No other can pout more and, therefore, it has the suitable name *Le Boudeur*, "The Pouty." Two anger bumps on the forehead and a short fat nose in a round face complete the whole expression. The doll number 252 always had sleep eyes and wig. It is possible for it to be placed on baby or toddler body; any other body would be incorrect. A few things should be known about the toddler body. It is a jointed body of a very small child which is starting to take its first steps. The torso is short and squat with a fat tummy. Arms and legs are also child-like corpulent with pronounced fat rolls on the inside of the thighs. A very cute detail is the spread out large toes. The doll number 252 is not exactly a rare doll. However, because of its popularity with collectors all over the world, this doll is not available in large numbers and, therefore, it is rather expensive.

As in the 1920s, the newborn baby, an infant as a doll became more and more fashionable, S.F.B.J. found themselves forced to offer these dolls. In 1928, *La Semaine de Suzette*, a magazine for small girls, announced the birth of *Bambino. Bambino* was an infant and smaller brother of *Bleuette*, a jointed-body doll from S.F.B.J. which the readers received as a present for their subscription. In each new magazine there were sewing suggestions for dresses and accessories — and now also a smaller brother, *Bambino*. It had a very good modeled baby body. The head was similar to that of the number 351 *Dream Baby* from Armand Marseille! It is so similar that the head was most likely delivered by them. Later infant dolls numbers 271 and 272 (marked "UNIS FRANCE") had different facial expressions and were rather rare.

Finally, one can say that the French doll industry to whom we owe a lot for their many inventions and developments, for example, the creation of the bébés and the development of the jointed bodies, also contributed a lot to the area of the baby dolls. French doll makers had earlier produced small child-like dolls. One also has to mention here the well-known Steiner doll with a mechanical clock-work in the body, *Bébé Gigoteur*, whose movements copied those of a kicking small child, or the Bébé Têteur from Bru which could drink out of a milk bottle and was delivered with baby clothing and a carrying cushion, very obviously meant to be a baby. S.F.B.J. produced and existed right up to 1957 but there were no other baby models made of bisque which are known to us.

S. F. B. J.
252
PARIS
11

The neck mark of the *Boudeur*, a sulking baby doll.

Baby doll in a walnut shell 2¹/₈in (5cm).

Leon Casimir Bru, Paris. *Bébé Têteur*, 8⅝in (22cm), circa 1885. It could drink out of a milk bottle.

S.F.B.J. Neck mark: "S.F.B.J. 251." Socket head, open mouth, sleep eyes, toddler body, 15³⁄₈in (39cm), circa 1915.

S.F.B.J. Left: Neck mark: "S.F.B.J. 236" Also called the *Laughing Jumeau*, 25⅝in (65cm).
Right: Neck mark: "S.F.B.J. 247." Called *Twirp*, 25⅝in (65cm). Both have socket heads, sleep eyes, open-closed mouths with two molded upper teeth. Left has a toddler body. Right has straight leg baby body. Circa 1915, old clothing.

S.F.B.J.: *Le Boudeur (Sulking Baby)* Neck mark: "S.F.B.J. 252 Paris 11." Socket head, light blue sleep eyes, closed pouty-mouth, red-brown original mohair wig original tod-dler body with ten joints, large upright toes, 23¼in (59cm), circa 1915, original sailor's suit.

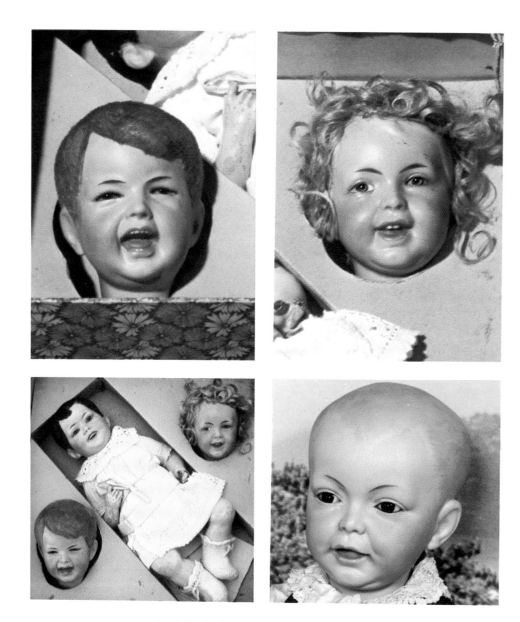

An S.F.B.J. Baby doll with three inter-changeable heads in original box. Above left picture: Number 233. Above right picture: Number 235. In box below left (center doll): Number 227.

Bottom right picture: Number 226. Socket head, fixed glass eyes, open-closed mouth, toddler body, 17¾in (45cm), circa 1915.

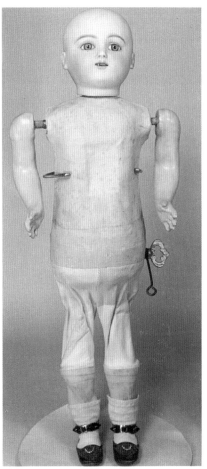

When the mechanism was wound up, the doll moved its arms and legs and called "Mamma."

Jules Nicholas Steiner, Paris: *Bébé Gigoleur* (mechanical baby). Marking on the mechanism: "J. Steiner Paris." Socket head, open mouth with upper and lower teeth (so-called "Vampire teeth"), 17³/₄in (45cm), circa 1878.

Baby Dolls in Museums

Up until a few years ago old dolls with porcelain heads had found no entrance into museums. Today, at least, they have come to be loved by all and are culturally valuable witnesses of past childhood and of contemporary history. They are finally being appreciated. Engaging persons (mainly former collectors) have been found who, with great personal and financial engagement, which often went far beyond their own means, have opened private museums. Suitable houses or rooms were found to take up these precious doll creations and their accessories of the same period and to give them fitting surroundings and present them in lovely arrangements. That is why we would like to present on these two pages private museums which greatly supported us with this book.

Above: Baby dolls in a newly opened Doll Museum Carin Lossnitzer, Coburg.

Below: Impressive arrangement in the Doll Museum Katherina Engels, Rothenburg o. Tauber.

Two lovely baby dolls in a rare chaise, Doll Museum Mathias Wanke, Limburg/Lahn.

A very enchanting scene in the Doll Museum Erika Steiner in Stein am Rhein (Switzerland), which is closed in the winter.

Reproductions

Reproduction of a boy doll marked only with "110." Some collectors believe that this doll is the missing number 110 of the character series from Kämmer & Reinhardt. Reproduction: Christel Kesting.

In the past few years a noticeable new branch of industry has developed. Along with it a new market for all the necessary materials to produce reproductions of old dolls has grown, from kilns to casting molds and porcelain clay to the complete accessories.

Collectors look at these new doll replicas with some apprehension and mistrust — apprehension because they are worried about their exclusive antique dolls, and mistrust, because they are concerned that these reproductions could be used at some time or another as a forgery. In connection with this, it is important first to think about how these reproductions came about. The reason for their creation was mainly found in the love and enthusiasm for the old dolls, whose radiance and fascination attracted a lot of collectors. Since the prices of the old dolls have risen so sharply in the last few years, a lot of collectors find it impossible to acquire the dolls to fulfill their wishes. Naturally, it is still possible to buy one or the other simple old doll. What should an inspired collector do when he or she falls in love, especially with an expensive *Hilda* or with an Oriental baby like Kestner's number 143?

So the idea was born to produce casts — and afterwards reproductions — of very special and beautiful dolls so that those who could not afford the antiques could own a reproduction of these small, otherwise unobtainable works of art. Other good reasons for the reproduction of old dolls are: first of all, it offers us the possibility that we can still enjoy dolls which we normally would never see, as for example, dolls from A. Marque, Bru, Jumeau, rare character dolls and still other rarities like the baby dolls which went as special orders to America. Besides, the number of available old dolls today would never be sufficient to cover the demands of admirers and collectors since the circle of collectors is continuously growing and the supply of old dolls grows smaller. In spite of all carefulness, it is unavoidable that some of these valuable objects are destroyed completely each year.

Therefore, courses have been and will be held so that the artistic skills of the reproduction techniques which are needed to produce good quality work are passed on. In order to make reproduction dolls of a high standard, good craftsmanship is required, as well as a steady hand, especially when painting. Not everyone is capable of this.

Especially talented women soon recognized that certain unforeseen possibilities were offered here. Not only had they found a lovely hobby, but they were also able to produce a wonderful collection of nearly all their favorite dolls. They could also work for others, by producing reproductions for further selling.

So far — so good! The problem is that the prices of these reproductions are often set too high. Instead, one should consider that the prices of reproductions should be in proper proportion to those of the old dolls, which today are already valued as antique and as mentioned previously, are getting fewer year by year.

Naturally, it is not said that every old doll should be generally more expensive than a reproduction, but instead each should be individually and very precisely differentiated. Since there are also large differences among the old dolls — which often occurred with the same dolls, so there are also large differences among reproductions. If one looks at a cross section of a lot of reproductions, one recognizes that there are original replicas and mass-produced replicas. A reproduction can be rather amateurishly made, but it can also be a small masterpiece, referring to the handicraftsmanship on one side and the artistic talent on the other. It begins with the porcelain casting, is expressed especially with the fine painting and ends with the handmade wigs as well as the exclusive clothing. That is why all of these facts should be expressed with the appropriate price differences.

Concerning forgeries, these were always found in all lucrative areas, as for example with paintings, jewelry, stamps, and so forth. This would only be profitable with expensive dolls, for example Bru, A. Marque, character dolls and rare baby dolls. It would take too much skill and time to produce an accurate copy and only a few could be offered for sale, because a large number offered would be rather conspicuous and, above all, the prices would sink. With a certain amount of special knowledge, one can protect oneself against frauds in that one does not purchase the expensive dolls under the table, but instead from specialized dealers or private persons where the origin of the doll can be traced back. A written guarantee of authenticity is a further step of protecting oneself.

"Singing" Heubach, 1987, 11¾in (30cm). Reproduction: Christel Kesting.

In principle, all reproductions should be signed with initial and year made.

"CK 1986" — signature of a reproduction made by Christel Kesting.

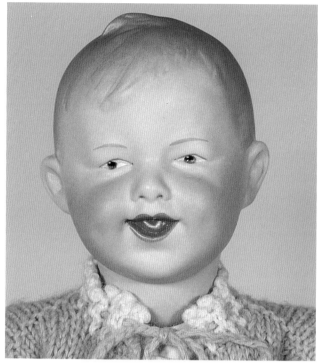

Above left: *Tynie Babe*, reproduction 1986, 7¹/₈in (18cm). Original baby doll on page 26.

Above right: Heubach reproduction, 14¹/₂in (37cm).

Below left: *Twirp*, reproduction 1986, 18¹/₂in (47cm), S.F.B.J. number 247. Original doll on page 92.

Below right: *Baby Love*, reproduction 1986. Original baby doll on page 72.

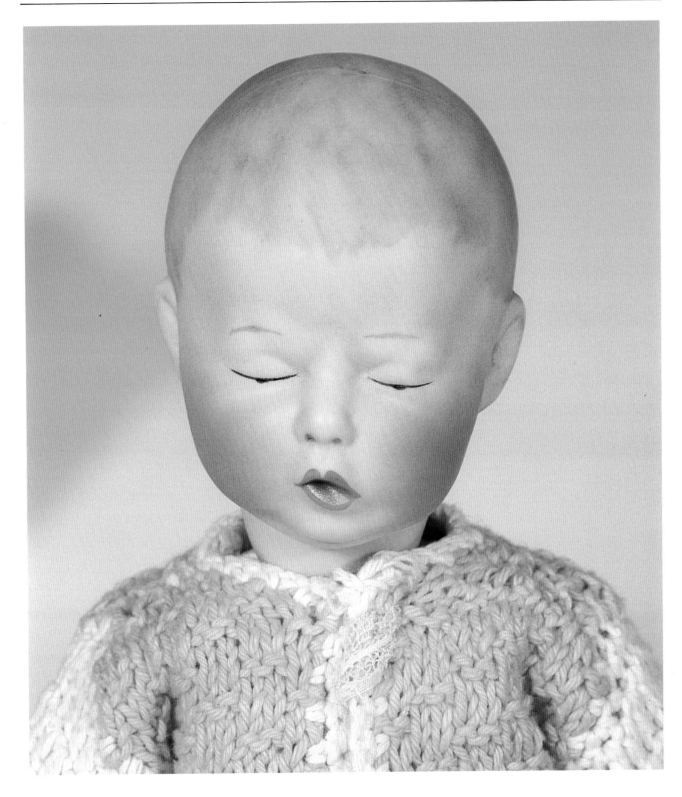

Heubach reproduction, 11in (28cm).

Above left: *Baby Gloria*, reproduction 1986, 13¾in (35cm). Original baby doll was produced by Armand Marseille circa 1920.

Above right: *Tynie Babe*, reproduction 1986, 11in (28cm). Original was made for E. I. Horsman Co., New York (see page 26).

Bottom left: *Baby Bo Kaye*, reproduction 1986, 13¾in (35cm). Original was made for Borgfeldt, New York, in 1926. Designer: Joseph L. Kallus.

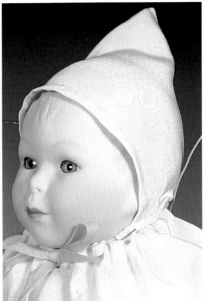

Fly-Lo, reproduction 1986, *The Little Aero Baby*, 9⅞in (25cm). Original made for Borgfeldt in 1928. Design: Grace Putnam. Clothes copied from the originals.

Above: Half-profile of *Fly-Lo*.

Below: *Lori*, reproduction 1986, 17³/₄in (45cm). Original produced by Swaine & Co.

◀ Page 102, below right: *Gladdie*, reproduction 1986, 15³/₄in (40cm). Original made for Borgfeldt in 1928. Copyright by Helen W. Jensen.

WAX DOLLS

Dolls made out of wax were produced a long time before china and bisque dolls. A great number of these wax dolls never survived the passage of time. Those who did survive had either missing noses or limbs. Most of all, they had small cracks in the wax, and more often than not they were discolored, which robbed the doll of its original beauty. Collectors with historical knowledge as well as museums are hardly moved by such criterion.

Picture on right: Wax doll (an infant to be baptized) with so-called "Motschmann-type" body: in fantastic condition, glass eyes, 13in (33cm).

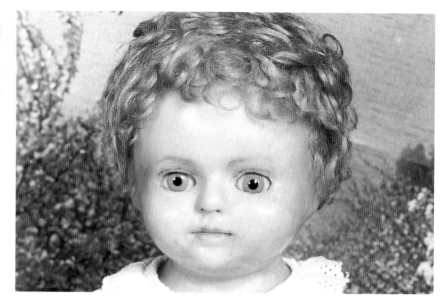

WOODEN DOLLS

Below left: a very early and rare wooden doll, glass eyes, with a so-called "Motschmann-type" body, 13³/₈in (34cm).

Picture on right: wooden doll, head covered with a layer of Gesso, bent-limb baby body made of wood with four joints, right hand balled into a fist, right arm strongly bent, 18⁷/₈in (48cm).

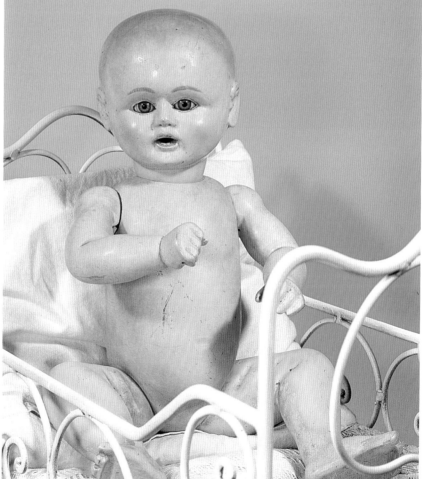

CLOTH DOLLS

Käthe Kruse's beloved dolls were developed using a very special method, invented by her, which made history. Many layers and impregnations made these (cloth) dolls relatively resistant, so that the title (friendly toy) was very precise. Opposite picture shows two *Traumerchens (Dreamers)*, 19⅝in (50cm), which are highly desired by all collectors. In the richly illustrated book *Doll Album 31 (Käthe Kruse Dolls)*, all known dolls are described.

CELLULOID DOLLS

Celluloid dolls became to be loved by all because they were inexpensive and due to the fact that there are so many various creations made by Schildkrot. Opposite picture shows a 4⅞in (12cm) baby doll marked with a Schild-krot trademark.

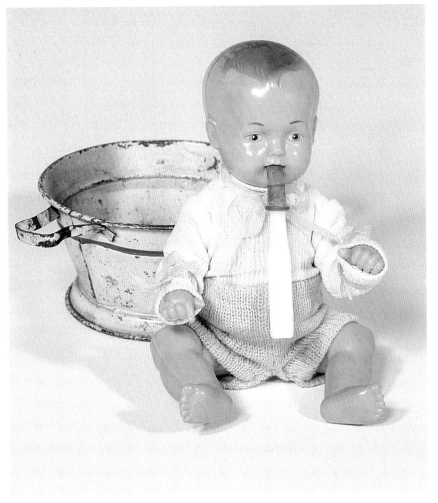

STONEWARE

A cute baby doll made out of so-called stone-ware, used especially for baby-care courses.

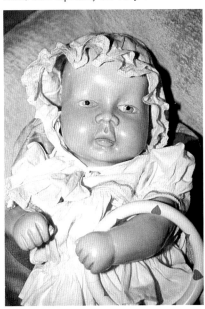

Baby Artist Dolls

Dolls were always made at all times — just like today. Even though this book is mainly dedicated to the antique baby dolls, it is still worth mentioning where the doll makers of today stand. Representing much other talent, a few outstanding artist doll makers are very clearly seen whose different styles are introduced on these two pages. Selfstating hobby, bound with success due to exhibitions and announcements in newspapers, on radio and television are continuous motivations for their constant creativity. Quite often this is followed with commercial success. For those who would like to know more about the making of such dolls, we recommend referring to the book *Artist Dolls* by Joachim F. Richter (Laterna Magica).

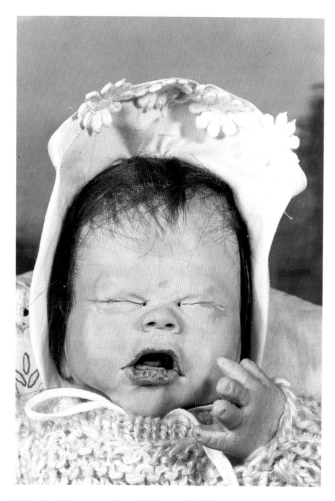

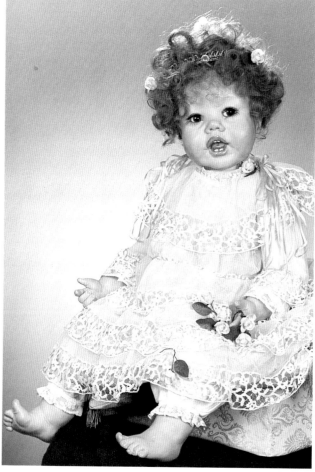

Rolanda Heimer produced this wonderful realistic (new-born) baby doll.

Carin Lossnitzer has already made a name for herself with her baby dolls, and the picture above shows one of her loveliest creations, a *Shirley Temple*-type.

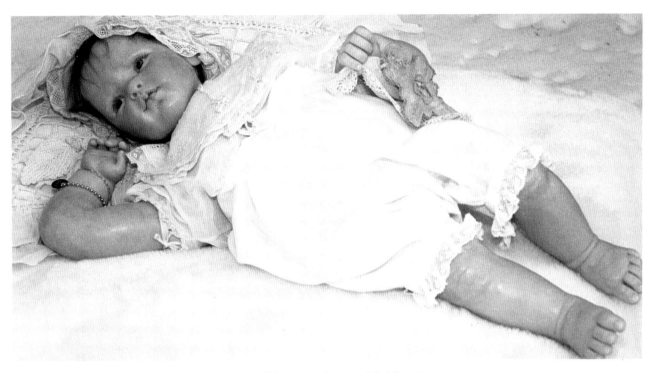

The well-known and successful doll artist,
Rotraut Schrott, produced this lovely baby
doll made out of Cernit.

Hildegard Günzel, who is rather successful at
international exhibitions, produced the doll
pictured here from bisque.

Baby Doll Clothing

It is the greatest pride of every collector to have one lovely old doll with its original clothing and, if possible, in its original box. It is, therefore, a great pity that this wish cannot be granted to a lot of collectors, since dolls in their lovely original clothing are far too rare and expensive for many collectors to enjoy owning. If one does have a doll which does not wear original clothing, the question arises, "How should it be dressed and what should it have on?" Before all doll collectors turn to this important matter of clothing, here are a few tips.

Original doll clothing. This term is meant for the factory clothing in which a doll was originally dressed and sold. A doll in its own original clothing is the highlight of every collection and, as well as ideally and financially seen, more precious than without clothing. For this reason it should never be changed. After all, the future generation would still like to see how such a doll looks in its original condition. The expensive baby dolls were often offered for sale in extravagant long clothes with a matching bonnet, often in a basket or on a baby pillow, or in a cute playsuit. The less expensive ones were often sold with only a baby shirt.

Black babies were often clothed in the same way as the white babies or they had very lovely, fanciful and colorful clothing, often copied after the style of the respective national dress. Small black babies were dressed in a grass skirt, with which they wore colored glass pearls or a wooden pearl necklace as well as earrings. At that period the clothing was made not only in the factories, but in cottage industries by seamstresses who mostly used sewing machines. However, several items were still sewn or knitted by hand. Only when one has seen a lot of original clothing does one recognize it again. A cloth, which was thin and often gauze-like, was used for the clothing of the white babies and a fine lace was used for the trimmings and extensions, tiny buttons and other suitable doll material.

For the exotic babies, solid or patterned silk or cotton materials, very often richly decorated with embroideries, edges or trimmings (sometimes made of silver or gold thread, tassels, pompons, cords and similar things) were mainly used. It would be perfect to dress a doll in original clothing which came from another doll which had either been lost or which had fallen apart. Naturally, these clothes are very desirable. Often one has to search for a long time at doll conventions, auctions, antique shows or shops and flea markets or

Oriental baby doll number 243 from J.D. Kestner in beautiful old clothing.

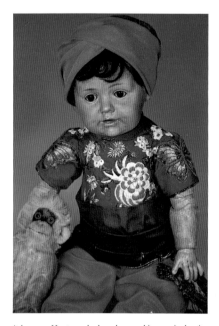

A brown Kestner baby, dressed in copied original clothing, made of silk: upper part hand-embroidered. This is how an original *Hilda* baby was found in the original box with the inscription "Orange devil".

from other collections in order to possibly find something and such clothing is usually quite expensive. The buyer should take utmost care that the clothing comes from the same period as the doll to be dressed and that the sizes and styles are befitting.

Old baby doll clothing. This is understood to be the clothing which was made at approximately the same time as the baby doll, but was produced later by the family or by a seamstress. These are also sought after and every collector is happy when they find beautiful old and sometimes hand-sewn clothing. Sometimes more pain and effort are taken to produce these than the industrial clothing, which often, in Germany, was described to be inexpensive and, as a rule, could never equal the precious French doll clothing.

Old baby clothing either sewn, knitted or crocheted — which once was worn by living babies is very suitable for the larger baby dolls. If someone was especially lucky, he could find and buy at the above mentioned places, precious baptismal dresses and bonnets at reasonable prices.

Copied baby doll clothing made from old patterns and from old materials would be the next most acceptable thing. One has to take into consideration — and that is the aim of this small clothing campaign — that this baby should be clothed the same as it had been when it was originally sold in the shop.

Today, models and patterns are no longer lacking and even old material can still be found. One can rummage eagerly in Grandmother's chest or at flea markets. Old underwear with delicate lace or fine embroidery is especially suitable for the clothing for the white babies. It would be a great pity if one cut up large but still good clothing. Torn or ragged pieces which still have firm parts of material should be used instead. Far more difficult is finding the appropriate old materials for the exotic babies. Pieces of old kimonos, either silk or cotton (from China or India) are very suitable, provided that the patterns are not too large and the colors are not too intense.

Baby clothing, as a rule, is not too difficult to make, which is often the case with the outer garments of the larger doll sisters. The larger doll's clothing was often subjected to the fashion of the time and sometimes sewn from very complicated patterns so that today, a lot of time is needed to copy such a pattern. Frequently this clothing was richly garnished with bows, hems, pleatings, frills or crimps, which is not to everyone's taste. So some collectors would often like to have the copied doll's clothing simplified, being of the opinion that dolls

Lace-decorated long dress with matching bonnet, suitable for copying.

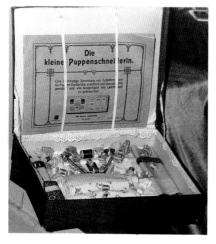

Sewing box, "The Little Doll's Dressmaker," pattern book, sewing thread, sewing needles, six different pieces of cloth patterned with flowers or plain, hooks and eyes, ribbons, lace and cloth flowers, 15³/₄in (40cm) by 19⁵/₈in (50cm), circa 1910.

with simpler clothing look far nobler. However, this elegant attire agreed with the fashions and taste of that time and it would be stylistically incorrect if one were to change this characteristic.

Copied baby doll clothing from old, stylish patterns and made from new materials is recommended for reproductions, but also, one can hardly refuse such clothing today for the old dolls, as long as one chooses similar materials to those used when the dolls were manufactured. Today these are again produced also for the old dolls using, for example, wool, cotton and silk materials as well as velvet ribbons, narrow lace and wide net lace, silk flowers and small embroideries. All these lovely trims which existed in Grandmother's time are again today often produced by hand and sold at doll conventions. If one does not find the right old fabric, one should look for suitable new material. There is no sense in using old material which falls apart in your hands when dressing your dolls, wasting the time and money invested. Chinese and Indian shawls and clothes of cotton and silk with small patterns and soft colors are more suitable for Oriental babies.

Clothing made from synthetic materials should not be used for old dolls and reproductions. One should refuse them — even an old pattern does not help. When dressed in synthetic fabrics, these dolls loose their nostalgic charm which has made them so lovable to us.

If one has made such a mistake, then one should not get upset, but learn from this mistake. Every child doll can have a few dresses for changing and also have something copied and made for its trousseau. The main thing is that the fun with this hobby will last for a very long time.

Index